The Clinical Interview

The Clinical Interview offers a new perspective on the patient encounter. Interpreting decades of evidence-based psychotherapy and neuroscience, it provides 60 succinct techniques to help clinicians develop rapport, solicit better histories, and plan treatment with even the most challenging patients.

This book describes brief skills and techniques for clinical providers to improve their patient interactions. Although evidence-based psychotherapies are typically designed for longer specialized treatments, elements of these psychotherapies can help clinicians obtain better patient histories, develop more effective treatment plans, and more capably handle anxiety-provoking interactions. Each chapter is brief and easily digestible, contains sample clinical dialogue, and provides references for further reading. These skills help clinicians practice more effectively, more efficiently, and with greater resilience. Whatever your clinical specialty or role, whether you are a trainee or an experienced clinician, *The Clinical Interview* offers practical wisdom and an entirely new way to think about the clinical encounter.

The Clinical Interview will be of great use to any student in a health-related field of study or a healthcare professional interested in refining their interviewing skills. It will help anyone from emergency medical technicians, nurses, and physician assistants, to nurse practitioners and physicians to build more meaningful patient relationships.

Scott A. Simpson, MD, MPH, is Medical Director of Psychiatric Emergency Services at Denver Health Medical Center and an Associate Professor at the University of Colorado School of Medicine. Dr. Simpson has advanced the treatment of behavioral emergencies through clinical practice, scholarship, and program development. A practicing emergency psychiatrist, he appreciates the unique challenge and privilege of working with patients and families in crisis. He lectures frequently across the country and has numerous peer-reviewed publications. Dr. Simpson is board certified in psychiatry, consultation-liaison psychiatry, and addiction medicine.

Anna K. McDowell, MD, is a psychiatrist and Co-Director of the Depression Consultation Team at the Rocky Mountain Regional Veterans Affairs Medical Center. As clinical faculty at the University of Colorado School of Medicine, Dr. McDowell teaches students, residents, and clinical staff. She is passionate about treating patients with complex mood, anxiety, and personality disorders and integrates multiple psychotherapeutic modalities in her patients' treatment. Dr. McDowell has formal training in dialectical behavior and psychodynamic psychotherapies and is board certified in psychiatry and addiction medicine.

"*The Clinical Interview* is a highly practical and user-friendly guide to the clinical application of evidence-based psychotherapeutic techniques to enrich the patient-clinician encounter. When patients feel heard, history taking is smooth, troubling thoughts and feelings are easier to elicit, and treatment planning becomes a team approach. Drs. Simpson and McDowell elegantly display a variety of psychotherapeutic approaches through the use of patient vignettes. This book will be a valuable tool to clinicians at all levels of experience."

—**Jagoda Pasic, MD, PhD,** Professor of Psychiatry, University of Washington

"Even the best clinician will walk out of the occasional clinical encounter thinking, 'Well, that could have gone better,' but still being unsure just what we could have done differently with our interviewing technique or brief interventions. *The Clinical Interview* gives readers a quick refresher of basic and advanced approaches to common and complex scenarios. It reads easily with brief and digestible tutorials which can be read quickly between clinical encounters or absorbed at length. A worthy addition to the library of any mental health clinician, new or experienced."

—**Jack Rozel, MD, MSL,** President, American Association for
Emergency Psychiatry, Associate Professor of Psychiatry and
Adjunct Professor of Law, University of Pittsburgh

"In this eminently practical and insightful book, written in plain English, Drs. Simpson, McDowell, and their colleagues offer helpful strategies and techniques that address key aspects of the clinical interview. These wise guiding principles and techniques will assist clinicians at all levels—from novices through experts—learn, reflect on, and call upon a huge variety of important 'tricks of the trade,' helpful for building and maintaining better alliances, treatment plans, and therapeutic interactions."

—**Joel Yager, MD,** Professor, Department of Psychiatry,
University of Colorado School of Medicine

"This book provides guidance to a wide range of providers who deal with patients that run the spectrum from mundane to difficult. This textbook is a recommended read for all."

—**Leslie S. Zun, MD, MBA,** Medical Director, Lake County Health
Department, Chairman and Professor, Department of Emergency
Medicine and Psychiatry, RFUMS/Chicago Medical School

"*The Clinical Interview* is a terrific compilation of top experts providing a kaleidoscopic study of varied aspects of psychiatry's backbone, the clinical interview. The well-structured format of individual concepts should make this an inviting read, and an invaluable resource, for students and seasoned professionals alike."

—**Scott Zeller, MD,** University of California, Riverside, Editor of
Emergency Psychiatry: Principles and Practice and
The Diagnosis and Management of Agitation

The Clinical Interview

Skills for More Effective Patient Encounters

Scott A. Simpson, MD, MPH and
Anna K. McDowell, MD

Routledge
Taylor & Francis Group

NEW YORK AND LONDON

First published 2020
by Routledge
52 Vanderbilt Avenue, New York, NY 10017

and by Routledge
2 Park Square, Milton Park, Abingdon, Oxon, OX14 4RN

Routledge is an imprint of the Taylor & Francis Group, an informa business

Library of Congress Cataloging-in-Publication Data
Names: Simpson, Scott A. (Scott Alan), 1982– author. | McDowell,
    Anna K., author.
Title: The clinical interview : skills for more effective patient encounters /
    Scott A. Simpson and Anna K. McDowell.
Description: New York, NY : Routledge, 2019. | Includes bibliographical
    references and index.
Identifiers: LCCN 2019008802 | ISBN 9781138346475 (hardback : alk.
    paper) | ISBN 9781138346505 (pbk. : alk. paper) | ISBN 9780429437243
    (ebook)
Subjects: MESH: Interview, Psychological—methods | Mental
    Disorders—diagnosis | Professional-Patient Relations | Medical
    History Taking | Communication
Classification: LCC RC473.D54 | NLM WM 143 | DDC 616.89/075—dc23
LC record available at https://lccn.loc.gov/2019008802

ISBN: 978-1-138-34647-5 (hbk)
ISBN: 978-1-138-34650-5 (pbk)
ISBN: 978-0-429-43724-3 (ebk)

Typeset in Minion
by Apex CoVantage, LLC

For Cora

Contents

Note: Chapters without listed authors were written by Scott Simpson and Anna McDowell.

Foreword

Where Art Meets Science

The phrase "the art of medicine" used to disturb me, especially when applied to psychiatry and behavioral health. It appeared to imply that psychiatry was "squishy medicine" and not based on science.

Many years and an appropriate number of gray hairs later, I finally understand what this phrase means. It fits psychiatry exactly. It is not a limitation but rather a phrase of respect for the less tangible tools necessary for our work. This book is a perfect example of the concept. A textbook chapter on the basic clinical interview would take fewer than 10 pages; even hitting all aspects of a bio-psycho-social history is a technically simple endeavor. Yet to master these things is another thing entirely. How do you capture accurate information while building a treatment relationship, engendering trust, and becoming a partner in the patient's care? When you progress beyond the most simple elements of the interview and begin understanding what it means to actually help patients . . . the art of medicine becomes real.

Human beings come in all shapes and sizes, with tremendous variation in background and experiences. Interview techniques that resonate for some will fall flat for others. Some techniques sound masterful from one clinician yet feel forced when used by another. One size does not fit all. Thus, this book nicely and succinctly presents a myriad of styles to interview a myriad of patients. In short, this book offers a colorful palette from which clinicians can learn to become artful interviewers.

Drs. McDowell and Simpson have a passion for teaching that is obvious in the creation of this book. Complex concepts are made easy to understand, and examples are given such that this text is useful for clinicians both novice and experienced. From initial approaches to advanced interview techniques, the information presented here is useful in virtually every clinical setting.

Enjoy your lesson in the art of medicine.

Kimberly Nordstrom, MD, JD
Medical Director for Behavioral Health, Colorado Access
Associate Clinical Professor of Psychiatry, University
of Colorado School of Medicine

Preface

Every healthcare professional has formative moments in training: their first correct diagnosis, their first thankful patient, their first tragic outcome. These events shape how we think about ourselves as clinicians and healers. From these experiences, some inherit a passion to tackle particular diseases like cancer or mental illness. Others want to care for a certain patient population—kids, veterans, or seniors.

As these formative moments are revealed, we are guided by our role models. Any trainee can describe great supervisors whose combination of technical skill, finesse with patient interactions, and mentorship were particularly inspiring. These mentors are the goal to which we aspire, and our work with them influences our careers. The importance of these role models is anecdotal but also backed by evidence. For example, medical students' choice of specialty is heavily influenced by the quality of their first clerkships in medical school.

One critical skill we learn from these role models is the ability to relate to patients. These mentors share with us which questions elucidate a diagnosis, how to explain a procedure, and how to form a trusting therapeutic relationship that will endure bad news, difficult treatment decisions, and great successes. These clinicians model a generous spirit and cultivate therapeutic relationships. And they make it look easy!

Over time, the details of those initial experiences fade. We come to recall those mentors not as infallible but instead as strong albeit imperfect clinicians. Our views of medicine grow nuanced; skepticism and burnout creep in. But chances are, you still recall how you felt when you first saw that great clinician connect with a patient, when you saw clinical care practiced the way you imagined it could be.

In this book, we hope to help every healthcare professional re-create the ease with which we all recall those great role models interacting with patients.

Contributors

Jonathan Buchholz, MD, Medical Director, Inpatient Psychiatry, Veterans Affairs Puget Sound Health Care System, and Assistant Professor, University of Washington School of Medicine, Seattle, WA

Vivian Cheng, PharmD, Pharmacist, Rocky Mountain Regional Veterans Affairs Medical Center, Aurora, CO

Jeffrey Clark, PharmD, BCPP, Pharmacist, Rocky Mountain Regional Veterans Affairs Medical Center, Aurora, CO

Heidi Combs, MD, MS, Medical Director, Inpatient Psychiatry, Harborview Medical Center, and Associate Professor, University of Washington School of Medicine, Seattle, WA

Ashley Curry, MD, Psychiatric Emergency Services, Denver Health Medical Center, Denver, CO, and Assistant Professor, University of Colorado School of Medicine, Aurora, CO

Amy Dowell, MD, Medical Director, Opal: Food + Body Wisdom, and Courtesy Clinical Instructor, Department of Psychiatry and Behavioral Sciences, University of Washington School of Medicine, Seattle, WA

Thom Dunn, PhD, Professor of Psychological Sciences, University of Northern Colorado, Greeley, CO, Clinical Instructor, University of Colorado School of Medicine, Aurora, CO, and Staff Psychologist, Denver Health Medical Center, Denver, CO

Alexia Giblin, PhD, CEDS, Executive Director and Co-Founder, Opal: Food + Body Wisdom, Senior Clinician, Radically Open Dialectical Behavior Therapy, and Clinical Faculty, Department of Psychology, University of Washington, Seattle, WA

Rachel Glick, MD, Clinical Professor, Department of Psychiatry, University of Michigan Medical School, Ann Arbor, MI

Alex Kipp, MD, MALS, Family Medicine Physician, Rosewood Family Health Center, Portland, OR

David Kroll, MD, Director of Clinical Care Redesign, Department of Psychiatry, Brigham Health, Boston, MA

Lindsay Lebin, MD, Chief Resident for Inpatient and Consult-Liaison Psychiatry, University of Washington School of Medicine, Seattle, WA

Edward MacPhee, MD, Section Chief for Psychiatry, Veterans Affairs Eastern Colorado Health Care System, and Associate Professor of Psychiatry, University of Colorado School of Medicine, Aurora, CO

Jesse Markman, MD, MBA, Associate Chief of Staff (interim) for Mental Health, Veterans Affairs Puget Sound Healthcare System, and Assistant Professor, University of Washington School of Medicine, Seattle, WA

Erin O'Flaherty, MD, Program Director, High Acuity Recovery Team, Rocky Mountain Regional Veterans Affairs Medical Center, and Clinical Instructor, University of Colorado School of Medicine, Aurora, CO

Lionel Perez, MD, Psychiatry Resident, University of Washington School of Medicine, Seattle, WA

Melanie Rylander, MD, Departments of Internal Medicine and Psychiatry, and Medical Director, Adult Inpatient Psychiatry, Denver Health Medical Center, Denver, CO, and Associate Professor, University of Colorado School of Medicine, Aurora, CO

Sarah Schrauben, MD, Child Psychiatrist, Western Psychological and Counseling Services, Portland, OR

Joleen Sussman, PhD, ABPP, Geropsychologist, Rocky Mountain Regional Veterans Affairs Medical Center, and Clinical Instructor, University of Colorado School of Medicine, Aurora, CO

Thida Thant, MD, Consultation-liaison Psychiatry Services and Assistant Professor, University of Colorado School of Medicine, Aurora, CO

Jodi Zik, MD, University of Colorado School of Medicine, Aurora, CO

Introduction

A New Approach to the Clinical Encounter

When training, we are so often overwhelmed with learning technical facets of medicine that we fail to learn how to maintain the treatment alliance at the heart of the profession. This observation is not meant to diminish the importance of evidence-based expertise—mastering these core skills is paramount to being a safe, successful, and effective clinician. But upon learning so much, passing certification examinations, earning licensure, and achieving the milestones of independent practice, many clinicians are left disappointed. They struggle with difficult patients who seem unappreciative or non-adherent. They feel impatient and overwhelmed. They feel that medicine is not what it should be and that they have fallen short of being a model clinician.

The result of these frustrations is burnout and dissatisfaction. There is an epidemic of burnout in medicine which stems in part from clinicians' inability to manage the clinician-patient relationship.[1-4] This relationship comprises a mismatch of high expectations and too little skills training. Our patients are sick, frightened, and overwhelmed. The language of medicine is foreign even among its practitioners, and contemporary healthcare systems are foreboding to navigate. Clinicians feel pressure by patients and administrators to ameliorate these problems in the space of ever-shorter appointments while being accountable to metrics for care quality and vague evaluations of patients' satisfaction. In this environment, there is too much pressure on all parties for ideal treatment relationships to form spontaneously and immediately. Everyone is doing their best—clinicians want to be helpful, and patients are earnest in wanting better health. Yet even under the best of circumstances, there are bound to be clinical encounters marked by irritation and disappointment.

Medicine does not need to be like this.

Most clinicians learn to conduct interviews and build therapeutic relationships through trial-and-error and mirroring their teachers. This ad hoc approach misses the opportunity to take advantage of a wealth of science behind effective clinical interviewing. There exists an incredible array of psychotherapies that are robustly studied, more effective than medications, and of utility for even severely ill patients. Many clinicians appreciate the value of therapy intuitively, but most forget how powerful a tool psychotherapeutic treatment is:

- Brief behavioral safety planning in the ED decreases the intensity of suicidal thoughts up to 6 months later[5] and decreases the risk of a suicide attempt up to a year later.[6]

1

- Dialectical behavior therapy decreases self-harm and suicide among patients with borderline personality disorder, one of the deadliest psychiatric illnesses.[7]
- Psychotherapy is the first-line treatment—before medications—for post-traumatic stress disorder.[8,9]
- Cognitive behavioral therapy is at least as effective as medications for treating depression, and its combination with medication treatment is more effective than either approach alone.[10]

All of these interventions are teachable and replicable. But while psychiatry is the field of medicine most dedicated to understanding the therapeutic relationship, psychiatrists have done a poor job adapting psychotherapy for the broader clinical community. The interviewing skills inherent to psychotherapy are often difficult to access for those who train outside mental health specialties. Delivering these therapies as originally designed requires specialized training by clinicians or expensive commitments by patients who attend frequent sessions. In practice, most psychiatrists use an eclectic mix of techniques from among various therapies—for example, starting with brief supportive therapy to validate the patient's ego strength, teaching mindfulness to manage episodes of anxiety, and implementing elements of behavior therapy to advance functioning. This adaptability is only possible after advanced training and experience with particular treatment modalities. Clinicians outside behavioral health are rarely given the time to learn different psychotherapy models and become sufficiently proficient to improvise in this fashion. Even in exceptional cases like motivational interviewing, the ongoing supervision and teaching for clinicians to achieve mastery is difficult to access. Training in specialized psychotherapies, such as dialectical behavior therapy or interpersonal therapy, are often unheard of outside of the mental health specialties.

The inability to translate what we have learned from evidence-based psychotherapies to wider clinical practice is a disappointment for a healthcare system founded on the working relationship between patients and clinicians. Clinicians feel disconnected from patients; patients feel misunderstood by clinicians. Too many clinical encounters feel regimented, rushed, and ineffective. The benefits of psychotherapy remain poorly disseminated, despite more patients than ever seeking psychiatric care. Patients do not even feel comfortable speaking up for their own safety.[11]

The aim of this book is to help clinicians create more effective treatment relationships with their patients through the application of evidence-based psychotherapeutic practices. Each short chapter describes a discrete interviewing technique that the healthcare professional can use to improve rapport, history taking, and treatment planning. These techniques are described in terms of their relationships to evidence-based psychotherapies and neuroscience. Techniques may be applicable for working with agitated patients, improving the quality of information gathering, or saving time in short encounters, among many other clinical situations. Admittedly this book is not for purists of psychotherapy; our goal is to make elements of psychotherapy accessible to a wider range of clinicians, practice situations, and patients. We believe the topic and format of this book is entirely unlike anything written to date.

In pursuit of this aim, be forewarned that this book contains frank depictions of the patient-clinician encounter. As with any human interaction, those between patients and clinicians are fraught with conflict, irritation, anger, and exhaustion (as well as laughter, camaraderie, generosity, and compassion). We provide neither blame nor excuses for bad decisions and rude statements made by both parties in the heat of the moment.

Rather we provide some context for why these bad interactions happen and empower clinicians to better handle these inevitable moments. When a clinician learns to handle these situations more effectively, they are more likely to feel proud of the care they have provided and less likely to suffer fatigue and burnout.

The techniques described herein are typically of two provenances. Some are specific strategies derived from well-established psychotherapies and adapted for a broader practice environment such as the primary care office or emergency department. Examples of these core psychotherapies include motivational interviewing,[12] cognitive behavioral therapy,[13] dialectical behavior therapy,[14] psychodynamic therapy,[15] and acceptance and commitment therapy.[16] Another group of techniques are learned from colleagues and not clearly grounded in a specific psychotherapeutic discipline. For this latter group, we explore the neuroscience and evidence that underlies their utility.

To demonstrate as varied a repertoire as possible, we recruited a diverse corps of contributors to write chapters in addition to our own. Most chapter authors are psychiatrists whose experience covers outpatient practices, community mental health, hospitals, and emergency rooms. Other authors are outpatient internists, hospitalists, psychologists, and pharmacists. What all these authors have in common is a belief that clinicians and patients alike deserve a more satisfying and more effective clinical encounter.

Our Intended Audience

We hope that any healthcare professional can benefit from this book—physicians, nurses, social workers, pharmacists, students, any clinician with regular patient contact.

The background provided is appropriate for advanced trainees in medicine and other healthcare fields. This text is not about basic interviewing skills—the reader should already know how to capture elements necessary for a history, diagnosis, and whatever information their role requires. Being familiar with those basics opens the door for the reader to apply the techniques described in this book to improve their interview skills, troubleshoot challenging patient encounters, and gain mastery in genuinely relating to patients. Chapters more focused on discussions of psychiatric complaints nevertheless recognize the frequency of such issues across primary care and non-specialty settings.

A Note on Language and This Book's Title

Language matters, and our use of certain terminology in this book reflects a larger philosophy towards patient care.

We use the terms "clinical" and "clinician" throughout this book to reflect the complexity of the interaction between the healthcare professional and the patient. Clinical practice is an extraordinarily nuanced undertaking. Only in simplest terms can it be described to involve a skilled practitioner and an ill patient seeking services. Clinical implies a constant consideration of a cost-benefit analysis weighing interpretation of scientific literature, financial costs to the patient and healthcare system, and ethical implications of those decisions. Clinicians must also be practical and modify treatments to their patients' preferences, needs, and abilities. The clinical interview involves a process by which all these aspects are considered in the service of building a treatment alliance, obtaining the necessary information for diagnosis and decision-making, and executing treatment. Clinicians are granted the privileges of medical knowledge and empowered by law to do things that most people cannot—perform surgeries, prescribe medications, or involuntarily detain sick patients. Many clinicians' training to do all these things is subsidized by government. Given this investment of power, position, and money by our larger society, clinicians are indebted to share their skills generously and justly.

More than do terms like "provider," "practitioner," or "healthcare professional," clinician evokes all these complex considerations. And "physician" is too literally limited for the range of clinicians working in the modern healthcare environment.

Just as the use of the word clinician is deliberate so too is our use of the word "patient." Various other terms have been proposed to describe the recipients of clinical services—client, consumer, person-in-recovery, among others.[17,18] If a particular patient prefers one of these terms, of course we have no issue using it with them. But to our mind, patient describes not only the circumstance of the person seeking services but also an active obligation by the clinician. Patient implies that a person is in distress and in need of the expertise available to the clinician who has an obligation to provide treatment. The term recognizes the inequities of knowledge and status inherent between the clinician and patient and places the burden on the clinician to take responsibility for these imbalances. The expectation to care for a patient is profound and universal; even in war, military clinicians care for enemy combatants. Moreover, patients are people whereas clients and consumers could interchangeably refer to companies and other corporate constructs. Clinicians do not care for corporations; they care for people to whom they are bound to give their best service without doing harm. The patient deserves treatment regardless of ability to pay, adherence to recommendations, or prognosis. Patient is the term that best reminds us of clinicians' obligations to respect their autonomy, desires, and personhood.

Finally, the title of the book incorporates the term "effective." What is an effective patient encounter? For the clinician, an effective encounter not only involves the application of successful treatment but also proves efficient and fulfilling in a way that protects the efficacy of the clinician for other patients. For the patient, an effective encounter includes recovery of function and avoidance of harm. All these successes depend on a trusting and working relationship between the clinician and patient.

How to Use This Book

This book is organized differently from most medical texts. Its organization is designed to make the material accessible to readers who lack psychiatric training. Chapters are succinct and deliberately organized. Chapters begin with "Setting," a common patient scenario describing when a technique might be helpful. Then, the technique is described and demonstrated in a short excerpt of conversation. (None of these examples are from actual patient encounters, and any resemblance is purely coincidental.) The final two parts of each chapter, "Why This works" and "Final Thoughts," describe why this technique is effective based on evidence-based psychotherapies and neuroscience; offer more guidance as to how the technique might be incorporated into the interview; and share hard-earned wisdom about avoiding pitfalls or anticipating problems in the technique's application.

Chapters in the book are organized based on a typical chronology of the patient visit: building rapport, taking a history, making an assessment, and planning treatment. This organization is somewhat contrived, as most techniques could reasonably be useful across multiple parts of the clinical encounter. For instance, the techniques in Section I, "Building Rapport," focus on building clinical relationships including with difficult or reticent patients, yet some rapport-building also happens when soliciting a history or developing a treatment plan. Similarly, the process of using the techniques in Section IV, "Planning Treatment," will inevitably affect the clinician-patient relationship. The sections are merely intended to help the reader better imagine how these techniques may be applied during the encounter.

Each chapter stands on its own. One might read straight through, starting and stopping at will, selecting techniques to try based on what sounds intriguing or relevant. Or one might read a chapter, then practice the technique a few times before moving on. Many of these techniques can be combined. Some of them represent different approaches to the same patient problem. For example, several different approaches are describing for working with upset patients. Another way to organize this book would have been by common patient scenarios. If you prefer to use the book as a reference for dealing with a particular situation, Table 0.1 organizes chapters based on their usefulness for certain patient presentations. All chapters are listed, some more than once:

Table 0.1 Techniques applicable to common patient situations

When working with a patient who . . .	*Consider using this chapter:*
Is uncertain what they want	1, 4, 6, 18, 34, 44, 47, 52, 57
Is difficult to direct or disorganized	1, 10, 19, 22, 23, 25, 26, 27, 28, 42, 44, 47
Is reluctant to work together	2, 3, 4, 7, 14, 20, 21, 24, 28, 29, 35, 37
Is anxious, worried, or upset	2, 3, 6, 8, 10, 11, 13, 33, 36, 59
Is angry	5, 8, 13, 16, 17, 33, 54
Is demanding	5, 15, 53, 54, 55
Brings up negative feelings in the clinician	9, 11, 12, 15, 16, 17, 33, 53
Worries they will never get better	14, 18, 34, 38, 43, 52, 59, 60
Has an unclear diagnosis	18, 19, 29, 30, 31, 32, 35, 39, 41
Is an unreliable historian	20, 21, 23, 25, 26, 27
Has a difficult time changing their behavior	31, 38, 40, 43, 44, 45, 46, 48, 49, 50, 51, 56, 57, 58, 59, 60
Does not take medications regularly	40, 41, 45, 49, 55
Has difficulty planning ahead	50, 51, 56, 58

Conclusion

Being a clinician is hard work. Being a patient is harder. We hope that this book serves as testament to the privileges and challenges of the clinician-patient relationship and strengthens our ability to make that relationship more fulfilling, satisfying, and effective for all involved.

References

1. Aiken LH, Clarke SP, Sloane DM, Sochalski J, Silber JH. Hospital nurse staffing and patient mortality, nurse burnout, and job dissatisfaction. *JAMA*. 2002;288(16):1987–1993.
2. Shanafelt TD, Noseworthy JH. Executive leadership and physician well-being: nine organizational strategies to promote engagement and reduce burnout. *Mayo Clin Proc*. 2017;92(1):129–146.

3. Dewa CS, Loong D, Bonato S, Trojanowski L. The relationship between physician burnout and quality of healthcare in terms of safety and acceptability: a systematic review. *BMJ Open.* 2017;7(6):e015141.

4. Ishak W, Nikravesh R, Lederer S, Perry R, Ogunyemi D, Bernstein C. Burnout in medical students: a systematic review. *Clin Teach.* 2013;10(4):242–245.

5. Bryan CJ, Mintz J, Clemans TA, et al. Effect of crisis response planning vs. contracts for safety on suicide risk in U.S. Army soldiers: a randomized clinical trial. *J Affect Disord.* 2017;212:64–72.

6. Miller IW, Camargo CA, Jr., Arias SA, et al. Suicide prevention in an emergency department population: the ED-SAFE study. *JAMA Psychiatry.* 2017;74(6):563–570.

7. Cristea IA, Gentili C, Cotet CD, Palomba D, Barbui C, Cuijpers P. Efficacy of psychotherapies for borderline personality disorder: a systematic review and meta-analysis. *JAMA Psychiatry.* 2017;74(4):319–328.

8. Lee DJ, Schnitzlein CW, Wolf JP, Vythilingam M, Rasmusson AM, Hoge CW. Psychotherapy versus pharmacotherapy for posttraumatic stress disorder: systemic review and meta-analyses to determine first-line treatments. *Depress Anxiety.* 2016;33(9):792–806.

9. Department of Veterans Affairs, Department of Defense. VA/DOD clinical practice guideline for the management of posttraumatic stress disorder and acute stress disorder: clinician summary. *VA/DoD Clinical Practice Guidelines 2017;* 2017. Accessed online December 20, 2018: www.healthquality.va.gov/guidelines/MH/ptsd/VADoDPTSDCPGClinicianSummaryFinal.pdf.

10. Cuijpers P, Berking M, Andersson G, Quigley L, Kleiboer A, Dobson KS. A meta-analysis of cognitive-behavioural therapy for adult depression, alone and in comparison with other treatments. *Can J Psychiatry.* 2013;58(7):376–385.

11. Fisher KA, Smith KM, Gallagher TH, Huang JC, Borton JC, Mazor KM. We want to know: patient comfort speaking up about breakdowns in care and patient experience. *BMJ Qual Saf.* 2018;28(3).

12. Miller WR, Rollnick S. *Motivational Interviewing: Helping People Change.* 3rd edition. New York, NY: Guilford Press; 2013.

13. Beck JS, Beck JS. *Cognitive Behavior Therapy: Basics and Beyond.* 2nd edition. New York, NY: Guilford Press; 2011.

14. Linehan M. *Cognitive-Behavioral Treatment of Borderline Personality Disorder.* New York, NY: Guilford Press; 1993.

15. Nestadt G, Di C, Samuels JF, et al. The stability of DSM personality disorders over twelve to eighteen years. *J Psychiatr Res.* 2010;44(1):1–7.

16. Hayes SC, Luoma JB, Bond FW, Masuda A, Lillis J. Acceptance and commitment therapy: model, processes and outcomes. *Behav Res Ther.* 2006;44(1):1–25.

17. Deber RB, Kraetschmer N, Urowitz S, Sharpe N. Patient, consumer, client, or customer: what do people want to be called? *Health Expect.* 2005;8(4):345–351.

18. Neuberger J. Do we need a new word for patients? Lets do away with "patients". *BMJ.* 1999;318(7200):1756–1757.

I
Building Rapport

1
Elicit One Goal
Be More Efficient by Learning the Patient's Agenda

Setting

Clinicians are busy. Healthcare systems demand productivity through short outpatient appointments and ever-present pressure to discharge from the hospital or emergency department. On one hand, this productivity maintains access to care for more people. But clinicians are challenged to maintain a focus on any individual patient. The resulting haste would come across as rude in any other human interaction: the average clinician does not ask the patient their goals for the appointment and interrupts the patient after 11 seconds.[1] Clinicians must balance efficiency with the need to understand the patient's goals in a compassionate, thorough manner.

The Technique

Elicit the patient's one most important goal at the outset of the appointment with an open-ended question. Patients who provide multiple, competing goals should be asked to prioritize their needs for the appointment, after which the patient and clinician may negotiate what secondary issues can be covered in the available time. When patients have difficulty identifying a single goal, ask for a short list of possibilities and the patient's best guess as to the most important item. The clinician can then ask the patient why they think that one item would be the most important to address.

Sample Dialogue

Patient: I have so much going on—my stomach is upset, and my back is really hurting. My sleep feels off a little, too. And I need refills for my medication. I think that's all, but maybe not!

Clinician: That does sound like a lot! What is the one most important thing that we should discuss today?

> Just one thing? I have a whole list!

> I imagine we can talk about much of this, but let's prioritize what is most important to you in the time we have.

> I guess the one thing I really need is a medication refill. But then if we have time, let's talk about my stomach.

> OK, the most important thing we need to discussion is your medication refill. Then your stomach issues. And then we can work on those other issues or schedule another appointment if we need. What made you think the medication refill is most important?

> Because if I don't take my medications, my blood sugars get really high, which is dangerous.

Why This Works

Interrupting the patient early does not make the encounter more efficient.[2] Early interruptions make it more likely that the patient brings up new concerns later in the visit or that their most significant concern goes unaddressed entirely. Eliciting the patient's one most important agenda item early on enables the clinician to anticipate how to spend time during the encounter and best address the patient's preeminent needs. Most patients are able to prioritize their needs, and they will communicate quickly. Left uninterrupted, patients disclose their agenda in an average of 6 seconds.[1]

If early interruptions don't save time, opening with the wrong questions does not, either. Opening an encounter with vague, open-ended questions such as, "How are you today?" is helpful in building rapport but inefficient in assembling a clinical agenda. The sample dialogue lays out clear ground rules for this encounter: What one thing is most important to discuss? Even quite ill patients are good at triaging their own medical needs,[3] and for some conditions self-triage is as accurate as that done by a professional.[4] Notwithstanding the need for clinicians' expert judgment in urgent cases, following the patient's lead in agenda-setting generally improves efficiency and safety.[5]

Many patients have multiple complaints as in the sample dialogue. The clinician can validate the patient's concerns and distress before reframing the agenda. The clinician is not closing any doors to the patient's concerns—only opening doors more selectively. Patient-centered communication demands that clinicians consider patient's preferences in addressing medical needs but does not abrogate the need for clinical effectiveness.[5] In the absence of a unifying diagnosis accounting for myriad complaints, the clinician needs to address a number of concerns and will only be able to do so with some control over the encounter's agenda. Neither solely adopting the clinician's priorities nor proceeding with an unfocused appointment benefits the patient.

Furthermore, this technique simplifies the patient's treatment goals. When a patient presents with so many concerns, the clinician is soon as overwhelmed as the patient. Clinicians can alleviate themselves of this burden by sharing responsibility for the encounter's agenda with the patient. Identifying goals is an important part of life but does not come easily for everyone. (After all, some persons seek therapy because they have difficulty understanding their personal and professional goals.) Understanding the patient's choices is helpful in planning further treatment; in this sample dialogue, it is clear that the patient has a sense of the dangers of medication non-adherence. In a sense, this technique is a variant of the technique described in chapter 47, except that the time horizon for the patient's goals is the end of the encounter rather than several weeks out. Both techniques are designed to aid in forming concrete priorities for treatment.

Final Thoughts

Identifying and pursuing the patient's agenda improves patient satisfaction, a common metric used in many healthcare systems' quality and pay-for-performance programs.[6] Clinicians often feel that trying to address satisfaction and productivity while maintaining safety is a losing battle. Remember also that follow-up encounters will not necessarily follow the same agenda as the first initial visit.[7] Clinicians should be prepared to re-examine the patient's goals every encounter. Patients whose desired treatment goals are unrealistic may benefit from a discussion around agenda setting (chapter 34).

References

1. Singh Ospina N, Phillips KA, Rodriguez-Gutierrez R, et al. Eliciting the patient's agenda-secondary analysis of recorded clinical encounters. *J Gen Intern Med*. 2018;34(1):36–40.
2. Hashim MJ. Patient-centered communication: basic skills. *Am Fam Physician*. 2017;95(1):29–34.
3. Miyamichi R, Mayumi T, Asaoka M, Matsuda N. Evaluating patient self-assessment of health as a predictor of hospital admission in emergency practice: a diagnostic validity study. *Emerg Med J*. 2012;29(7):570–575.
4. Eijk ES, Busschbach JJ, Monteban H, Timman R, Bettink-Remeijer MW. Towards patient self-triage in the ophthalmic emergency department: sensitivity and specificity of a self-triage instrument. *Acta Ophthalmol*. 2014;92(7):697–700.
5. Institute of Medicine (US) Committee on Quality of Health Care in America. *Crossing the Quality Chasm: A New Health System for the 21st Century*. Washington, DC: National Academy of Sciences; 2001.
6. Boissy A, Windover AK, Bokar D, et al. Communication skills training for physicians improves patient satisfaction. *J Gen Intern Med*. 2016;31(7):755–761.
7. Rey-Bellet S, Dubois J, Vannotti M, et al. Agenda setting during follow-up encounters in a university primary care outpatient clinic. *Health Commun*. 2017;32(6):714–720.

2

Validate Three Different Ways

Be Authentic in Your Validation by Expanding the Ways in Which You Can Agree With the Patient

Setting

Validating patients' feelings and thoughts are an essential part of building a treatment alliance. Successful validation requires the clinician to be authentic—even when you do not entirely agree with the patient. It is important to be adaptable while interviewing in order to deliver effective validating statements.

The Technique

The simplest form of validation is to agree with what the patient is saying. When this proves too difficult, the clinician can agree with how the patient is feeling about a situation. And if that does not feel authentic, validate the likelihood that any patient would feel similarly given the circumstances.[1]

Sample Dialogue

Patient: You are not treating me fairly. I don't think you care about me at all!

Clinician: I understand that you feel you are being mistreated.

Do you? Because you don't act like it.

I think anyone who felt they weren't getting what they needed would feel like they were being treated unfairly. And I understand that you feel this way. But I do not feel comfortable prescribing that medication for you.

> Well, then perhaps I just need to see a different doctor.

> I can appreciate why you would want to see someone else. Let's talk about the treatment options I *can* offer you.

Why This Works

What is validation, and why is it important? Validation is the act of affirming a person's viewpoint, including how they think and feel. Giving validation is a way of giving value to others' opinions, perspectives, and decisions. For the patient, hearing validating statements reminds them of their own self-worth and personal value. Our need for validation begins at a young age, when our caregivers provide affirmation of our basic needs, thereby reminding us how our own opinions and wants matter. Across cultures, persons who grow up without the validating support of loving caregivers are prone to anxiety and interpersonal difficulties later in life.[2,3]

As important as validation is for the clinical encounter, validating statements should always be delivered by the clinician from a genuine, authentic position. False affirmation is easily detected by the patient. Patients who have a history of trauma are often highly sensitive to inauthentic validation, and upon hearing it become upset.

The clinician is thus in the position of having to find some way to validate the patient's stance without appearing inauthentic even in situations when there is disagreement. In the sample dialogue, the patient posits that they are being treated unfairly. The clinician of course disagrees so cannot honestly repeat back that statement as the simplest form of validation. (It would not work to reply, "You are being treated unfairly.") Rather, the clinician acknowledges the patient's sense of being mistreated—surely the patient does feel that way, and it is hardly a stretch for the clinician to agree with that sentiment. The patient then escalates to a more provocative statement to which the clinician validates the likelihood that any patient in that position would feel similarly. Again, a sensible statement of fact. Validating this fact also serves to normalize how the patient is feeling.

Validation serves an important role for the clinician throughout the interview. Validation is an important part of verbal de-escalation.[1] It can also be used to better direct the clinical interview (as described in chapter 22). Generally, delivering validating statements humanizes the patient and begins building a clinical relationship that can buffet bad news and difficult decisions. In this example, the clinician provides validating statements to de-escalate the patient and improve the likelihood of a sensible treatment plan.

Final Thoughts

Clinicians have a hard time agreeing with upset or angry patients. This difficulty stems from clinicians' own sense of invalidation wrought by the patient. The patient's position may make the clinician feel worthless, inept, or unvalued. These feelings interfere with the clinician's ability to respond with validating statements. Yet it is the clinician's ability to return authentic validation to the patient that will ultimately resolve these negative feelings in the clinician and improve the clinical encounter for both parties.

References

1. Richmond JS, Berlin JS, Fishkind AB, et al. Verbal de-escalation of the agitated patient: consensus statement of the American Association for Emergency Psychiatry Project BETA De-escalation Workgroup. *West J Emerg Med.* 2012;13(1):17–25.
2. Keng SL, Wong YY. Association among self-compassion, childhood invalidation, and borderline personality disorder symptomatology in a Singaporean sample. *Borderline Personal Disord Emot Dysregul.* 2017;4:24.
3. Zweig-Frank H, Paris J. Parents' emotional neglect and overprotection according to the recollections of patients with borderline personality disorder. *Am J Psychiatry.* 1991;148(5):648–651.

3

Mirror the Patient's Language to Build Rapport

Use the Patient's Phrasing to Avoid Misinterpretation

JODI ZIK, MD

Setting

While gathering information, formulating a working diagnosis, and developing a treatment plan during an interview, it can be difficult to find space to develop a personal connection with the patient. One barrier to developing this connection is the clinician's use of medical jargon. Patients may feel unheard and misunderstood when clinicians lean on obscure words and professional terminology. Reflecting a patient's story by using their own words engenders the comfortable environment necessary for patients to reveal intimate details and better partner in their care.

The Technique

Use the patient's language whenever possible. For example, if a patient describes dissociative episodes as "the times when I am erased from the story," use this exact phrase to elicit other accompanying symptoms. Though clinicians may need to mentally categorize patient's statements into signs and symptoms necessary to make a diagnosis, the interview should be a shared experience of exploration and understanding between the patient and the clinician.

Sample Dialogue

Clinician: What changes or sensations have you noticed in your body since you were diagnosed with diabetes?

Patient: I have these zaps in my fingers and toes. It always feels like I'm wearing mittens when I try to pick things up, so I stopped taking the medication because I figured that was the problem.

I'm glad we were able to have this conversation. Those zaps are actually caused by damage to your nerves by too much sugar.

Oh! My sugars are causing the zaps?

Exactly. Diabetes leads to excess sugar in your body, and that's causing the zaps. Taking your medication regularly every day will improve them and prevent them from getting worse.

Why This Works

When a patient's words are constantly molded into a preset list of medical terms—"anhedonia," "neuropathic pain," or "delusion"—the patient's personal experiences risk being trivialized, leaving both the patient and the clinician unsatisfied. Utilizing the patient's language is a quick and easy way to develop rapport and enhance understanding between clinician and patient. The average American reads at an 8th grade level,[1] and patients often do not understand medical terminology.[2] Nevertheless, many clinicians fall into the habit of using healthcare jargon and complicated language when explaining diagnoses and treatments. This communication divide alienates patients and inhibits open, honest communication.

For the patient, understanding a clinician and feeling understood are not synonymous. Even when treating more educated patients, clinicians communicate more effectively by adopting the patient's language. Research in cognitive pragmatics, or the study of the mental states of people interacting with each other, suggests that people communicate based on patterns of shared social knowledge.[3] People within a group, whether that group is based on culture, religion, or shared experiences, develop a communal knowledge base which they use to connect to one another. A detailed understanding of the intricacies of medicine is rarely communal in the physician-patient relationship. Allowing a patient to share the nuances of their experience in their own words allows the clinician and patient to begin creating their own shared knowledge base, which in turn leads to a more genuine and meaningful connection.

Interviews can quickly become rote and boring when the clinician merely searches for a symptom inventory and diagnostic criteria, over and over, while disregarding any information deemed extraneous. This technique re-engages the clinician in the clinical interaction by compelling attention to the patient's words. Even more concerning, if we throw away the patient's words, we lose the opportunity to understand the patient more deeply and guide treatment more effectively. In the sample dialogue, it is important to identify when a patient is experiencing diabetic neuropathy, but the patient is more likely to be invested in the diagnosis and treatment plan if it is explained to them using their own language about how their body feels. Mirroring the patient's language allows the patient's formulation of themselves to be heard, which in turn leads them to share more of their story and be open to the clinician's thoughts. The interaction grows more rewarding and effective for both the clinician and the patient.

Final Thoughts

This technique can be used with any patient. Regardless of one's education level or medical knowledge, being a patient is a vulnerable role. Sharing language helps patients feel more comfortable revealing details of their life, which in turn leads to more accurate diagnoses and realistic treatment plans. Some clinicians fear that if they do not re-define a patient's story in medical terms, they cannot make a good diagnosis. In fact, effective communication between physician and patient has been correlated with improved treatment adherence[4] and overall health outcomes.[5]

The principal pitfall in using this technique is mirroring language whose meaning is unclear or whose use hinders treatment. Ask the patient to clarify their statements if you do not understand what they mean or you need more detail. Perhaps the clinician in this sample dialogue needs more detail about what the patient means by "zaps." Mirroring profanity or degrading another clinician can devolve the therapeutic conversation into one between peers rather than one between a healer and patient in distress. Even if sharing an informal comment can on occasion create an alliance with the patient, do not lose track of the goals of the clinical interview. This technique should always be used in a professional manner to best serve the patient's interests.

References

1. Doak CC, Doak LG, Root JH. *Teaching Patients with Low Literacy Skills.* 2nd edition. Philadelphia, PA: J. B. Lippincott Company; 1995.
2. Hayes E, Dua R, Yeung E, Fan K. Patient understanding of commonly used oral medicine terminology. *Br Dent J.* 2018;223(11):842–845.
3. Airenti G, Bara BG, Colombetti M. Conversation and behavior games in the pragmatics of dialogue. *Brain Lang.* 1993;17(2):197–256.
4. Zolnierek KB, Dimatteo MR. Physician communication and patient adherence to treatment: a meta-analysis. *Med Care.* 2009;47(8):826–834.
5. Stewart MA. Effective physician-patient communication and health outcomes: a review. *CMAJ.* 1995;152(9):1423–1433.

4
Use the Power of "And"
Introduce "And" Rather Than "Or/But" Statements to Your Interview to Establish Rapport, Validate the Patient's Experience, and Facilitate Change

ASHLEY CURRY, MD

Setting

Every day, clinicians help patients make difficult decisions and change unwanted behaviors. Change is more difficult when patients see their choices as an all or nothing affair—for example, when one choice is entirely positive and the other choice is entirely negative. This rigid, dichotomous thinking acts as a roadblock to solving problems and leads patients to feel helpless. In fact, most decisions are difficult and nuanced. Having a tool to identify and validate patients' ambivalence is invaluable in helping patients realize change.

The Technique

Identify the conflict that the patient is facing by listening for opposing viewpoints or desires. These are often easy to spot by the patient's use of the word "but" or the use of the word "or." Patients may say, "I *have* to do *x*, or else *y* will happen," or, "I want to do *x*, but I can't because of *y*." Patients may use these statements after you suggest something that they find judgmental or difficult to accomplish. Once the conflicting ideas are identified, repeat them back to the patient—using "and" instead of "but/or." Consider adding a statement that acknowledges the frustration (or confusion) of having two different feelings or thoughts simultaneously.

Sample Dialogue

> Patient: My sleep isn't getting any better. I've been trying the tips you suggested, but when I took the benzodiazepine at night, I slept so much better. But I know that's bad for me, too.

> Clinician: It sounds like you have really been trying to get better sleep. You're in a tough spot, because you can't help but think about how medications have helped you in the past, and at the same time, you want to get better sleep without the medications.

> Yeah. I know these other things you recommended are better for me, but I just feel so exhausted.

> That's understandable. I want you to get good sleep, too, and I want to make sure that you are doing it in the safest way possible. Treating insomnia takes some time and work. It is understandable to want to go back to using medication…and once these changes start to take effect, you'll see long-lasting benefit without risky side effects.

Why This Works

Many people are prone to dichotomous thinking and view a situation in absolute terms. Black-and-white thinking is frequently problematic among patients with anxiety, depression, and personality disorders.[1,2] Most things in life, however, exist on a continuum: rarely are circumstances all or nothing, strictly one or the other.

Because patients often assume clinicians are unilaterally opposed to anything that is bad for the patient, they hesitate to voice thoughts not in support of change. Patients fear these thoughts will be met with the clinician's judgment and disappointment. Clinicians can also fall into this trap of rigid thinking. It is easy for clinicians to focus on what is best for the patient and overlook how the patient's thoughts and emotions relate to their willingness to change. Once the clinician and patient identify with opposite sides of a position, both persons tend to double-down on their point of view. The resulting clinician-patient conflict disrupts rapport and stalls positive change.

"And" statements make it possible to validate two opposing viewpoints. The "or/but" conjunction negates the preceding sentiment, whereas the "and" conjunction gives equal importance to both choices. For example, "Smoking is bad for me, but I don't want to stop." This language reflects patients' sense that they must choose between two opposing options and be wholly committed to that choice. A perception grows that decision-making is simple and absolute, when in fact changing behavior is hard and requires ongoing work.[3] It can be true that, "Smoking is bad for me, and I don't want to stop." By using "and," the clinician diminishes harmful dichotomous thinking.[4] Here, the "and" statement re-affirms smoking's dangers and simultaneously acknowledges the patient's desire to continue smoking.

Using "and" statements also allows the clinician to identify conflict without conferring judgment. They demonstrate to the patient how both statements can have merit, and that one may both want and not want something simultaneously. Framing conflict in this manner affirms that it is okay to have contradictory points of view. We need not feel bad about doing or saying one thing while harboring thoughts and feelings to the contrary. This approach is valuable for building rapport, as patients will not get the impression that a viewpoint in opposition to their own is necessarily more valid or correct.

When discussing topics of change, motivational interviewing facilitators often first acknowledge the viewpoint that sustains current behavior and end the reflection with statements related to change. The sample dialogue demonstrates the clinician moving from acknowledging the appeal of current behaviors to supporting the patient's interest in change. By ending with statements of change, the patient is left with more recent thoughts of change and invited to further explore arguments in favor of changing behavior.

Final Thoughts

While this technique highlights the patient's dilemma, it does not resolve the conflict—only the patient can do that. You may find yourself in a position where the patient is asking for an outright answer. In response, validate the patient's conflict, take a non-judgmental stance, and offer yourself as a resource to the patient while he or she works through the conflict. This moment is an opportunity for another "and" statement that shares the clinician's own ambivalent position: "I would love to give you a simple solution to this problem, and I know that this is a decision you will have to make on your own. I will help in any way I can while you work through this."

References

1. Arntz A, ten Haaf J. Social cognition in borderline personality disorder: evidence for dichotomous thinking but no evidence for less complex attributions. *Behav Res Ther*. 2012;50(11):707–718.
2. Gebhardt C, Alliger-Horn C, Mitte K, Glaesmer H. All-or-nothing thinking: the processing of emotional expressions in traumatized post-deployment soldiers. *J Anxiety Disord*. 2017;47:69–74.
3. Miller WR, Moyers TB. Motivational interviewing and the clinical science of Carl Rogers. *Journal Consult Clin Psychol*. 2017;85(8):757–766.
4. Teasdale JD, Scott J, Moore RG, Hayhurst H, Pope M, Paykel ES. How does cognitive therapy prevent relapse in residual depression? Evidence from a controlled trial. *J Consult Clin Psychol*. 2001;69(3):347–357.

5
Redirect Demanding Patients
Reinforce That the Patient, Like Everyone, Is Entitled to Good Medical Care

Setting

Patients who are thought to be demanding or entitled often demonstrate unrelenting requests for physician attention and the "best of the best" care available. These patients sometimes use intimidation, devaluation, and threats to coerce the physician into ordering medications, tests, and treatments the patient feels necessary or even deserved. Patients who are very important persons, or VIP patients, sometimes fall into this category.[1] Demanding patients are challenging to work with and can engender fear, anger, and a sense of powerlessness in the clinician.

The Technique

When a patient is demanding specific tests or treatments beyond what is indicated, validate their concerns about their health and treatment. Then discuss how they are, like all patients, entitled to good medical care and that is what you will continue to provide. Threats made by the patient can be acknowledged but need not be challenged. If it feels appropriate, the clinician may ask the patient of what they are afraid: for instance, being ill, dying, or being uncared for by the clinician.

Sample Dialogue

Patient: You had better get me that new medicine! If you don't, I'll sue you for everything you're worth!

Clinician: It sounds like you really feel the new medicine will be helpful for you. I know you have been feeling poorly for some time, and I understand why you would want to try something else.

> Darn right, I read online that it's the best treatment! You'll be sorry if you don't prescribe it for me!

> I hear that you are upset. You deserve the best medical care we can provide to you, and I will continue to provide that. Let's talk about why this medication might not be the best for you. You are in a very difficult position, having struggled for so long. And maybe you fear that nothing will ever help.

Why This Works

This technique allows patients to voice their underlying fear, validates their concerns, and emphasizes their right to good medical care.

Why might a demanding patient act in this matter during a clinical encounter? The demanding patient may resent feeling overly dependent on the clinician. They may also be afraid.[2] Fears among demanding patients include a decline in health, abandonment by the clinician, or even death. In soliciting the demanding patient's fear, the clinician opens the door to a more genuine discussion of what will actually best serve the patient. Chapter 13 describes the association between anger and fear.

Validation's importance for de-escalating challenging patients cannot be overemphasized and again plays a role in this technique's efficacy.[3] Validation serves to acknowledge that the patient has been heard and understood. This alone often circumvents a charged situation. Validation is particularly important for demanding patients whose attacks or self-centeredness mask their own insecurities and fears.

Reminding patients that you are actually providing them with good care seems basic but is surprisingly effective in re-directing patients' demands. This statement validates their concern and easily aligns with their goals. It can be stated simply and authentically by the clinician. When spoken, this statement serves to reinforce the clinician's own confidence—which may be rattled by the accusatory patient. This approach moves the discussion away from whether quality care is being provided to what that quality care entails.

Counter-intuitively, VIP patients are at significant risk for sub-optimal care. These risks largely relate to misguided attempts to accommodate VIP patients' comfort and preferences. For example, standard procedures may be modified and safeguards made laxer. Inconvenient tests may be omitted. Or the opposite may happen: unnecessary tests are ordered for fear of missing something yet actually raise the risk of iatrogenic harm.[1] Redirecting the patient's entitlement towards what constitutes quality care helps focus the clinician and satisfy the patient.

Final Thoughts

Working with demanding or entitled patients can be challenging. A pitfall of this technique is the patient who cannot accept validation and redirection. These patients are usually quite upset or even emotionally dysregulated, and techniques to address these states are more likely to be helpful. If you feel unsafe or unable to think clearly in response to your patient's emotional state, consider whether it is better to end the encounter. You cannot provide good medical care, and the patient cannot receive it, when you are both distressed.

References

1. Frenklach A, Reicherter D. The treatment of VIP patients in academic teaching settings: applying the "difficult patient framework" to guide therapeutic response. *Acad Psychiatry.* 2015;39(5):597–600.
2. Greenberg L. Emotion-focused therapy: a synopsis. *J Contemp Psychother.* 2006;36(2):87–93.
3. Richmond JS, Berlin JS, Fishkind AB, et al. Verbal de-escalation of the agitated patient: consensus statement of the American Association for Emergency Psychiatry Project BETA De-escalation Workgroup. *West J Emerg Med.* 2012;13(1);17–25.

6

Be Silent

Use Active Silence to Support the Patient's Emotional Expression

JESSE MARKMAN, MD, MBA

Setting

To be a clinician is to share intimate and life-changing moments with patients. These moments are fraught with powerful emotions that can overwhelm both patient and clinician. In psychiatric visits, eliciting these emotions may be a goal of treatment, while in other settings these moments feel as though they derail the interview and therapeutic relationship. Regardless of the context, the clinician must effectively help the patient manage intense affect.

The Technique

Use active silence to support the patient in difficult moments. This technique is one of the simplest yet most difficult to use with a distraught patient. The actively silent clinician uses supportive body language—instead of words—to convey interest and empathy. Maintain an open posture while seated, and lean slightly forward, while keeping eye contact and a supportive facial expression. These expressions convey interest in and empathy to what the patient is saying without words. Space is left open for the patient to express themselves. Most patients will self-limit their own emotional expression and take the interview in a new direction or permit the clinician to transition to other topics. This transition is an opportunity for the clinician to validate what just occurred and reinforce the benefits of expressing the emotions the patient has been feeling.

Sample Dialogue

Patient: I have spent so much of this week missing her that I can't seem to do much else with myself.

Clinician: ...

> I just feel empty and alone…she used to push me to get outside of myself, and now I can't do that on my own. I miss her so much!

> ...

> I just want her back. I need to figure out how to get on with life.

Why This Works

Clinicians often feel pressured to act during the interview. This temptation to do *something* is particularly acute when the patient is struggling—as if the clinician must do something important or say something enlightening to make the pain disappear. A patient's fuming, crying, or yelling builds still more pressure to end this discomfort. Often, though, the clinical encounter is the patient's chance to be with those emotions in a safe space with another person present. Most patients spend the majority of their time around others who are uncomfortable with emotional displays. Sitting with a clinician who can demonstrate acceptance and empathy towards emotional distress validates that distress and its importance to the patient. Sharing emotional moments builds therapeutic rapport and demonstrates how feelings can be shared without judgment.

The space it affords to create this shared moment does not entirely explain the value of silence. Supportive and validating statements also meet these aims. What silence uniquely allows the distressed patient is the opportunity to explore their feelings without limits. Many interview techniques are meant to guide an interview, and in so doing these techniques place limits on the patient. These limits have a role in clinical encounters, but there is also value in the patient's exploration of their own distress in the safety of the clinician-patient relationship. In addition, the persistence of silence creates social pressure for the patient to speak, which will force the patient to further elaborate on their own feelings and history.[1]

Deep expressions of intense emotions are therapeutic. Patients often carry distress with them in their everyday lives but limit their expressiveness for fear of losing emotional control entirely. The sample dialogue illustrates a patient who is struggling with grief. Upon accessing some of these strong feelings, the patient's fear of this expression recedes. The patient explores just how sad they actually feel and what it is like to carry that sadness. As a result of this exploration, the fear of the severity of these emotions somewhat subsides. The patient has expressed this sadness and nothing bad has happened. Perhaps the clinician had a similar fear as the patient—a fear that the patient would "fall apart" as a result of exploring these feelings. In fact, failing to provide the opportunity for that exploration would have been unfortunate given the therapeutic resolution of this encounter.

Clinicians need not fear or avoid patients' emotions.[2] There is therapeutic value in simply sharing physical space with the patient. Palliative care nurses have reported that one of the most empathic and supportive things they can do for a patient is simply be with the patient as the patient feels what they are feeling.[3] Once the patient's most intense emotional expressions pass, the patient and clinician can discuss what just happened together.

One final benefit of this technique: patients practice self-limiting their emotional expression. Feeling such intense emotions quickly becomes suffocating but then soon diminishes, like a fire that consumes its own oxygen. That the patient can so quickly regain control is an important lesson, and the clinical encounter helps the patient realize a model for how these feelings can resolve. The patient learns the strength of their natural ability to cope and acquires confidence that better feelings will return. They may even engage in coping strategies (e.g., paced breathing or other grounding techniques that bring them back to the present moment), which the clinician can notice and highlight in order to remind the patient to utilize these skills in the future.

Final Thoughts

The active use of silence can feel very much like the clinician is doing nothing. In reality, the clinician is applying a difficult therapeutic skill and using less to accomplish more. One challenging aspect of this technique is learning when silence is appropriate and when different techniques should be used to manage intense affect. Often, starting with silence lets the clinician feel out the course and intensity of the emotional expression. But patients who cannot self-soothe may progress to become increasingly irritable, agitated, or uncontrolled and need more active verbal de-escalation by the clinician.

References

1. Buetow SA. Something in nothing: negative space in the clinician-patient relationship. *Ann Fam Med*. 2009;7(1):80–83.
2. Yalom ID. *The Gift of Therapy: An Open Letter to a New Generation of Therapists and their Patients*. New York, NY: HarperCollins; 2002.
3. Rydé K, Hjelm K. How to support patients who are crying in palliative home care: an interview study from the nurses' perspective. *Prim Health Care Res Dev*. 2016;17(5):479–488.

7

Be Playful

Introduce Playful Irreverence to Challenge Rigidity, Signal Affection, and Build Social Connection

AMY DOWELL, MD, AND ALEXIA GIBLIN, PHD, CEDS

Setting

Patients with overcontrolled temperaments display inhibited or disingenuous emotional expression, an aloof and distant style of relating to others, rigid and rule-governed behavior, and overly detail-focused and cautious behavior. Overcontrolled temperaments are often seen in patients with refractory depression, anorexia nervosa, treatment-resistant anxiety disorders, and obsessive-compulsive personality disorder.[1] This temperament introduces challenges for working together in a clinical relationship.

The Technique

Use playful irreverence during the interview. Playful irreverence employs warm and playful teasing by the clinician to challenge the patient's rigid thinking while signaling affection, warmth, and openness. One way a clinician might use this method is to jovially express disbelief to a contradictory or obviously fallible belief of the patient's. While gently teasing, the clinician uses nonverbal cues to reinforce an affectionate stance: evince a wry, cooperative smile with raised eyebrows, sit comfortably in your chair, consider a small shrug of the shoulders or an openhanded gesture.

Sample Dialogue

Patient: Mom is evil; she doesn't even care. She wouldn't let me go on an overnight trip last weekend with my friends, so we got in a huge fight.

Clinician: Rough. I wonder how come she didn't want you to go?

> She said it was because I haven't been eating and lost weight, and because I have been getting dizzy again, but I am sure it's because she doesn't want me to be happy. She always does this. She never says yes to anything.

> Wow, you say you have been dizzy and haven't been eating, and your mom was so worried about you that she took the weekend off to help make sure you were able to eat enough food? That same mom who you said was buying you a new car for school this year so you wouldn't have to walk? She does sound pretty evil.

> Well, when you say it that way, I guess she's not totally evil…just kind of.

Why This Works

Humans are by nature social creatures. We crave attachment, companionship, and belongingness. Excessive self-control inhibits a patient from experiencing these basic human wants. When a patient feels safe, liked, and connected with their clinician, they are more likely to be flexible and lighthearted. This connection in turns helps the patient move from a place of rigid inflexibility to one of willingness to consider alternative experiences. Playful irreverence signals to the patient that the clinician-patient relationship is a friendly one. After all, gentle teasing is something we tend to use with close friends and family. Using this technique with a patient demonstrates that you feel your relationship is strong and intimate enough to accommodate this playfulness. The clinician's use of this technique also models for the patient one way to develop social connectedness to others.

This technique works particularly well with patients who exhibit too much self-control and inflexibility. Overcontrol leads patients to be isolative and lonely with all persons including their clinician. Overcontrolled temperament poses an increased risk for chronic mental health issues.[1] In practice, patients with excessive levels of self-control often appear defensive when presented with treatment recommendations or respond to questions about how they are feeling with a superficial answer, for example, saying that they are "fine" or doing "okay." These responses rarely match with their underlying emotional state.

Gentle, warmhearted teasing lets the clinician challenge the patient's maladaptive behavior while also demonstrating warmth and care. In this dialogue, the clinician playfully challenges the patient's perception of her mother. The clinician balances confrontation with multiple affirmations in order to demonstrate that they are on "the patient's side." Teasing allows the patient to be more open to taking in feedback from the clinician without becoming defensive or shutting down. The clinician provides a model for playful conversation, and the patient is given room to experiment with responding to feedback with greater flexibility and openness. This technique is frequently used in Radically Open Dialectical Behavior Therapy (RO DBT), a psychotherapy designed for treating patients with overcontrolled temperaments. The goals of this treatment include increasing flexibility and decreasing emotional loneliness.[2,3] Because the overcontrolled patient typically takes life overly seriously, the clinical stance in RO DBT mixes playful irreverence and compassionate gravity.

Final Thoughts

Overcontrolled patients struggle with all social relationships, including with their clinician. These patients often feel an urge to exercise self-control when they perceive clinicians to be overly cautious, strict, or uptight. This technique is then particularly helpful as a social signal that the patient can express themselves safely and practice some of the skills necessary for alleviating loneliness, isolation, and distress. This technique helps the overcontrolled patient feel more connected to their clinician, encourages openness and flexibility, and aids more effective treatment.

References

1. Lynch TR. *Radically Open Dialectical Behavior Therapy: Theory and Practice for Treating Disorders of Overcontrol.* Oakland, CA: New Harbinger Publications; 2018.
2. Hempel R, Vanderbleek E, Lynch TR. Radically open DBT: targeting emotional loneliness in anorexia nervosa. *Eat Disord.* 2018;26(1):92–104.
3. Lynch TR, Hempel RJ, Dunkley C. Radically open-dialectical behavior therapy for disorder of over-control: signaling matters. *Am J Psychother.* 2015;69(2):141–162.

8

Handle the Hollering With a Calming Question

Through Tone of Voice, Active Listening, and Setting Limits, Invite a Conversation to De-Escalate a Shouting Patient

THOM DUNN, PHD

Setting

Clinicians regularly encounter patients whose emotions are running high.[1] Fueled by frustration, fear, or feelings that they are not being heard, some patients raise their voices. A shouting patient is a problem. Shouting is a clear sign of agitation, is disruptive to the clinical setting, provokes other patients, and can incite clinicians to respond in a counterproductive manner. The clinician's first approach to the agitated patient immediately sets the tone for de-escalation. Most agitated patients readily respond to verbal de-escalation.[1]

The Technique

Engage the patient with an introduction and a question, "What can I help you with?" Shouting is contagious, and it is easy for a clinician to also raise their voice, but the clinical interaction should not be a contest of who can talk louder. Listen carefully to the patient and anticipate when the patient will take a breath. During the brief lull afforded by the patient's inspiration, the clinician is able to interject, calmly and in a quiet voice, "Hold on, I want to make sure I understand what you are saying." Most people will stop talking so that they can listen to see if they are being heard. This opportunity lets the clinician reflect the patient's concerns and then direct the conversation. "I understand you are frustrated about having to wait so long. I am here to help, but I can't do that as long as you are yelling. Would you mind taking a few deep breaths so we can work together?"

Sample Dialogue

Patient: I'm leaving! Let me go or I'm calling a lawyer!

Clinician: My name is Dr. Smith, I am in charge here today. What can I help you with?

> Everyone lies here! No one cares about people! They said it wouldn't be very long, but I have been here all day.

> Hold on, I want to make sure I understand what you are saying. You have been waiting too long. You are feeling like no one cares that you are here. I appreciate that. We are doing our best to get to you, but yelling isn't helping. It is hard to understand what you are saying in this small space when you yell. Would you mind lowering your voice so we can talk and I can see what I can do to help?

> I've been here way longer than other people who are already getting to leave, it isn't fair.

> I understand that it feels like you are not being treated fairly. Some people's situations are different than others. We can work together, and I can figure out what is taking so long and give you some information.

> I'm not a bad guy, I don't mean to yell. I'm just scared.

Why This Works

Patients who raise their voices often do so because they feel like they are not being heard. These patients are likely to be in a negative emotional state such as feeling angry, afraid, or frustrated. It is not uncommon or surprising for clinicians to respond poorly to being on the receiving end of someone's yelling. Our natural response to being yelled at is often to yell back phrases like, "Calm down!" "You must be quiet!" and "Shut up!" These phrases are perceived to be disrespectful and dismissive of the patient's negative emotional state.[2] Such responses worsen a difficult situation and result in iatrogenic agitation, leading to the need for sedation or restraint—that is, they do not make the situation safer for anyone.[3]

A more effective approach is to interact with the agitated patient in a calm manner, employing a quiet voice that projects professionalism and empathy. In the sample dialogue, the clinician's introduction is concise and unambiguous. This initial engagement permits the clinician to demonstrate an empathetic understanding of the patient's situation and foster the patient's trust.[4] Engaging a patient while they are in a negative emotional state builds a powerful therapeutic alliance. The patient feels that they are being heard. The patient also has the opportunity to disclose what is contributing to their negative emotional state. In the example above, the dialogue closes with the patient saying, "I'm just so scared." This opening lets the clinician explore what is contributing to the patient's fear and what choices can help the patient feel less fearful.

Opening verbal de-escalation with an invitation—"What can I help you with?"—to the patient later allows the clinician to more effectively set limits on the patient's behavior. Agitated patients feel out of control and respond favorably to appropriate limit setting. The clinician should confidently inform patients that certain behaviors are not tolerated. Some staff worry about "rewarding" a patient who is shouting by paying attention to them. However, many patients will escalate their yelling if no one sets limits and engages in verbal de-escalation. Failing to engage the patient who is shouting sends the tacit message that "It's OK to yell here." What follows are profanity-laden statements, verbal attacks of a personal nature on staff or other patients, or a progression of agitation from verbal escalation to violence.

Returning to the sample dialogue, the clinician applies this technique to introduce gentle reassurances that the patient is safe, that he is going to be well taken care of, and that he is staying longer than others is not a sign that he is going to be "locked up." This technique thereby reduces the patient's fear. And the shouting.

Final Thoughts

De-escalation often requires some trial-and-error including repeating validating statements or an admission that the clinician and patient must "agree to disagree" (chapter 16). This technique does not replace sound clinical judgment about when a patient has become too agitated for a safe interaction. There are situations with particular patients for whom this technique is not effective. Sometimes the time for verbal de-escalation will have passed and, unfortunately, managing agitation requires medical or other interventions.[3]

References

1. Stene J, Larson E, Levy M, Dohlman M. Workplace violence in the emergency department: giving staff the tools and support to report. *Perm J.* 2015;19(2):e113–e117.
2. Thompson G, Jenkins, JB. *Verbal Judo: The Gentle Art of Persuasion.* New York, NY: HarperCollins; 1993.
3. Knox DK, Holloman GH. Use and avoidance of seclusion and restraint: consensus statement of the American Association for Emergency Psychiatry Project BETA Seclusion and Restraint Workgroup. *West J Emerg Med.* 2012;13(1):35–40.
4. Horvath AO, Luborsky L. The role of therapeutic alliance in psychotherapy. *J Consult Clin Psychol.* 1993;61(4):561–573.

9

Recognize Your Own Emotions

Identify and Process Your Countertransference During the Interview to Improve the Patient's Well-Being (and Your Own)

JONATHAN BUCHHOLZ, MD, LIONEL PEREZ, MD,
LINDSAY LEBIN, MD, AND HEIDI COMBS, MD, MS

Setting

Patient encounters can evoke strong emotions in clinicians. The clinician's emotional response to the patient, called countertransference, ranges widely in nature and intensity depending on the scenario. Consider the last time you were angry or frustrated with a patient. When feeling this way, it is hard to think and provide good care. Working with the patient while also managing these feelings is emotionally exhausting. Clinicians must be able to understand, identify, and manage countertransference in order to be effective with patients.

The Technique

During the encounter, take a moment to use three steps that help conceptualize countertransference:

1. *Intellectual understanding*: The first step in managing countertransference is recognizing that emotions will arise during patient interactions. Understanding countertransference as a concept helps explain our own inevitable emotions and behavioral responses during the clinical encounter. Unrecognized emotions lead to confusion, distress, and dissatisfaction in our personal and professional lives.
2. *Experiential awareness*: Be aware of your physical sensations, feelings, and thoughts during a clinical encounter. Peculiarities in your physical or mental state are important clues that countertransference is affecting the interaction. Is your heart racing? Are you holding your breath? Pay attention to your ability to think and your level of comfort in the encounter. Are you having difficulty diagnosing or treatment planning? Are you behaving differently than you would in other clinical encounters?
3. *Management*: This step is the natural result of the first two. Anticipating the possibility of a countertransference reaction and being aware of the reaction when it occurs enables the clinician to avoid untoward responses, problem-solve effectively, and demonstrate empathy. Cultivating empathy promotes mature coping skills, which in

turn reduces emotional distress. After the encounter, process what happened with a supervisor or colleague to normalize the experience and improve self-awareness.

Sample Dialogue

Patient: I'm so upset with this…I feel like I can't stop crying. I just can't handle this!

Clinician: *How can I help them stop crying? It's uncomfortable just sitting here like this. Maybe we just need to a new topic to discuss.*

This topic is really upsetting you. Why don't we talk about something else right now?

Patient: I can't…I just can't talk about anything else; why can't you see that!

This isn't going well, my heart is racing. I'm anxious just like the patient. I'm going to take a deep breath to calm down for a moment.

You're feeling really anxious and distressed right now.

The patient's taking a deep breath and calming down, too. I think they feel understood.

Why This Works

Understanding, identifying, and managing countertransference are core clinical competencies regardless of practice setting. Recognition and management of emotions in the clinical encounter improves both patient and physician satisfaction.[1]

Of note, countertransference happens at the earliest moments of clinical training: medical students experience unrecognized feelings toward patients during clinical encounters.[2] These feelings lead to problematic behaviors like avoidance or overcontrol that impair interview performance. Trainees quickly learn what types of patients induce these strong emotions—for example, mentally ill patients—and develop professional interests and biases in response.[3]

In the patient dialogue, the clinician initially attempted to shift the conversation away from the topic causing the patient's distress. This decision was informed by the clinician's unrecognized feelings of anxiety and distress. As the clinician's— and patient's—discomfort continues, the clinician begins to consider that they are experiencing a countertransference reaction (step 1). They reflect quickly on their own internal reactions to the patient and identify related inner feelings of anxiety and distress (step 2). The clinician then transitions to management by naming and validating the emotions experienced and using a deep, purposeful breath as a coping skill (step 3). This technique orients the patient emotionally and helps them feel understood and supported.

The connection between managing countertransference and clinical effectiveness is biologically sensible. Emotions are generated and managed through the brain's limbic system, which includes the amygdala, the part of the brain most strongly implicated in emotional processing. The limbic system in turn activates the autonomic nervous system. A clinician may feel confused or distressed by emotional countertransference, but the act of naming and processing emotions reduces their intensity: functional magnetic resonance imaging suggests that actively labeling affect decreases limbic system activity and increases higher-order cognitive functions.[4]

When recognized and processed, countertransference allows the clinician to gain a clearer sense of the patient's experience. If countertransference emotions are avoided, it is likely to worsen the clinician's experience of the encounter and potentially the quality of the care delivered. Unrecognized and unprocessed countertransference contributes to each of the three components of burnout—emotional exhaustion, cynicism, and decreased sense of personal efficacy. But actively working with countertransference restores a clinician's joy of practice.

Final Thoughts

Recognizing emotions in oneself during the clinical interview is challenging. Experiencing negative feelings about patients can conflict with the values of altruism that most clinicians hold dear. As such, you may be reluctant to be honest about your emotions or to express them in fear of being perceived as judgmental or not empathetic. Remember that every single clinician experiences these emotions and reacts to them. Furthermore, countertransference is a good tool to help maintain professional boundaries and duties to the patient. If during the process of managing countertransference you find yourself attempting to justify inappropriate or unusual clinical decisions, seek consultation with a trusted colleague.

References

1. Alfandre DJ. Do all physicians need to recognize countertransference? *Am J Bioeth.* 2009;9(10):38–39.
2. Smith RC. Teaching interviewing skills to medical students: the issue of "countertransference". *J Med Educ.* 1984;59(7):582–588.
3. Cutler JL, Harding KJ, Mozian SA, et al. Discrediting the notion "working with 'crazies' will make you 'crazy'": addressing stigma and enhancing empathy in medical student education. *Adv Health Sci Educ Theory Pract.* 2009;14(4):487–502.
4. Lieberman MD, Eisenberger NI, Crockett MJ, Tom SM, Pfeifer JH, Way BM. Putting feelings into words: affect labeling disrupts amygdala activity to affective stimuli. *Psychol Sci.* 2007;18(5):421–428.

10

Reflect the Patient's Statements
Use a Well-Timed Reflection to Disrupt a Negative Thought Spiral

JESSE MARKMAN, MD, MBA

Setting

Particularly when discussing difficult topics, patients may find themselves caught in a negative thought spiral. These spirals occur when the patient thinks about and discusses something troubling to the point of feeling very upset, which leads to more negative thoughts about other distressing topics, which leads to the patient feeling further upset, and so on. The negative thought spiral usually continues to feed back into itself and escalate as the patient's anguish increases. The clinician soon feels trapped in this spiral as well, not wanting to invalidate the patient by changing the subject but fearing that the patient will only grow more upset. The skilled interviewer can disrupt these negative thoughts to offer perspective on difficult topics and refocus the interview.

The Technique

Offer a reflection to stop the patient's negative thought spiral. A reflection is a declarative statement that summarizes and affirms the meaning of the patient's statements. Providing a reflection allows patient to feel the support of the clinician. In motivational interviewing, reflection is used to create a warm and empathic environment.[1] In this technique, reflection is used to break a thought pattern through an empathic action.

When working with a patient in good emotional control, a clinician may introduce a reflection at many different points. However, when interviewing a more dysregulated patient, the clinician should insert the reflection into the interview at the first sign of the patient losing emotional control. An early reflection breaks the flow of negative thoughts and statements, which would otherwise derail the encounter.

Sample Dialogue

> Patient: ...and he just left. He left me, and all I could think was how stupid I had been, and how it's all my fault, and how I should have taken more time and paid him more attention, and been a better...

> Clinician: You were extremely sad and frustrated.

> Exactly! I was, and I just wanted another chance. If I wasn't stupid and a waste of space, I would have seen things were going poorly months ago. Why was he interested in me in the first place!? Who is going to even take a second look at me at this point...

> This really shook your confidence and made you question yourself.

> When you put it like that, yeah, it really did.

Why This Works

This technique aims to disrupt an unimpeded flow of negative or distressing statements from the patient. This approach differs from the common approach of letting the patient take the interview where they want. In some clinical encounters, it may be appropriate or necessary to let the patient discuss these negative thoughts, and chapter 6 describes the use of active silence in these situations. But a negative thought spiral quickly becomes distracting and unhelpful to the encounter. A purposeful break is beneficial for the more dysregulated patient.

A reflective statement helps the patient pause and regain control of their emotional state. Presenting the break in conversation as a reflective and summarizing statement demonstrates the clinician's engagement in the interview. It does not appear to the patient that the clinician is seeking to stop the flow of conversation as much as it appears that the clinician is listening and engaging. This use of reflection brings the patient out of their current train of thought. A well-timed reflection encourages a pause, consideration, and response by the patient. Stopping to consider a reflection enables the patient to step outside of their experience and re-imagine it from the clinician's point of view. The patient must ask themselves, "Is what they just said accurate?" This change in direction diffuses the patient's affective state, allows for exploration, and empowers self-regulation.

It can appear that making this type of reflection places pressure on the clinician to be "correct" in their interpretation of what the patient means by their statements. This is not the case. In fact, a reflection has been described as merely a guess by the listener as to what the speaker means.[2] The guess may be correct, or it may not, but it does not greatly matter. A reflection containing an incorrect sentiment can be just as valuable as one with a correct sentiment. If the patient is required to stop and correct the clinician, this correction creates even more disruption to the negative thought spiral. The clinician might then thank the patient for the correction and making things clearer.

Final Thoughts

The most difficult aspect of applying this technique is inserting the reflection naturally so that the clinician's entrance into the conversation is welcomed and felt to be empathic. One way to achieve empathy is by using words and phrases that match the patient's. The clinician's synchrony with the patient's phrasing style increases perceived empathy.[3] Additionally, a reflection will be more effective when shared by the clinician with confidence. When the clinician is tentative, patients do not know how seriously to consider the clinician's statement. An upset patient may not even register what is being said if presented too timidly. Clinicians find more success with this technique when inserting reflections confidently.

References

1. Miller WR, Rose GS. Toward a theory of motivational interviewing. *Am Psychol*. 2009;64(6):527–537.
2. Miller WR, Rollnick S. *Motivational Interviewing: Helping People Change*. 3rd edition. New York, NY: Guilford Press; 2013.
3. Lord SP, Sheng E, Imel ZE, Baer J, Atkins DC. More than reflections: empathy in motivational interviewing includes language style synchrony between therapist and client. *Behav Ther*. 2015;46(3):296–303.

11

Introduce Progressive Muscle Relaxation
Give the Patient an Active Task to Change Their Emotional Experience

JESSE MARKMAN, MD, MBA

Setting

Sometimes, the patient's emotions become so intense that they cannot participate in the interview. Further conversation becomes impossible, and the clinician's soothing words are not enough. Patients even experience panic attacks or severe anxiety during the encounter. Clinicians need to be prepared to help the patient regain their composure and return to a place where they can participate in the encounter.

The Technique

Help the patient engage in progressive muscle relaxation during the visit. Progressive relaxation involves guiding the patient through a process of contracting and then relaxing muscles.[1] This exercise can be guided by the clinician, or both the clinician and patient can listen to a recorded exercise. If the patient is able to participate enough to give permission, ask if they would be willing to try the exercise together. There will be times when the patient is too dysregulated to engage in decision-making; when this is the case, simply start the exercise and ask the patient to follow along.

A written instruction sheet simplifies instruction for the clinician and can also be given to the patient to take home. After the patient visibly calms, debrief what just happened with the patient: How was the exercise helpful? How might the patient use it again in the future? A complete course of progressive muscle relaxation can take 15 minutes or longer, but shorter courses are also effective. The sample dialogue and Table 11.1 provide instructions for a short course of muscle relaxation.

Sample Dialogue

> Patient: I just feel so scared and alone when it happens. I have no control and I just feel like I am going to die.

> Clinician: I can tell that you are really upset right now. Are you feeling some of those panicky feelings?

38

...

Let's do an exercise together to bring us back to where we are right now. Let's start by scrunching up our toes and our feet as tight as we can for the next 10 seconds. I want to you contract all of the muscles you can feel in your feet as tight as you can. Feel what that feels like, and how your muscles begin to feel tired and burn. Now, as we get to the 10 second mark, relax the muscles in your feet as much as you can. Feel what it feels like to relax for the next 10 seconds. Notice the difference, and focus on releasing the tension…

Why This Works

When patients feel too distressed to participate in the interview, the clinician must help the patient abruptly change their emotional experience. One way to induce this change is by modifying the patient's physical sensations. A significant change in body physiology leads to emotional change.[1] This connection between the mind and body is harnessed in Dialectical Behavior Therapy (DBT). In DBT, distress tolerance skills help patients move away from a state of overwhelming distress into a state where cognitive skills may be accessed to manage emotions. Progressive muscle relaxation is a valuable distress tolerance skill.

In progressive muscle relaxation, the participant alternates between intense contraction of specific muscle groups and deliberate relaxation of those same muscle groups. The patient may focus on areas of specific tension or move gradually throughout the body, contracting and then relaxing each muscle group from head to toe. The simple and repetitive instructions are easy to follow and soothing to hear.

This technique is a tangible and pragmatic way to aid the distressed patient and bring them back to the present moment. Using this technique clearly leads to a break in the interview, but in this case the break is necessary and valuable. The break helps not only the patient but also the clinician who may similarly be feeling overwhelmed and helpless. Compared to more passive relaxation techniques such as focusing on deep breaths, progressive muscle relaxation is an active behavioral intervention. Passive techniques are sometimes insufficient to slow the racing thoughts and calm the intense emotions of a distressed patient. An active technique gives agency back to the patient and provides a skill the patient can use in the future. Once the patient relaxes, the clinician and patient can share a calmer moment, debrief, and resume the encounter.

This technique is part of a larger repertoire of mindfulness-based interventions. These interventions seek to cultivate mindfulness, or an awareness of current thoughts, actions, and the present moment. The practice of mindfulness has been shown to be effective in the treatment of a number of mental health conditions including anxiety and personality disorders.[2]

Final Thoughts

Many emotions arise in the clinician facing a distressed patient: worry, helplessness, frustration, and impatience. (Why is this patient upset? We have other things to discuss!) When patients become too upset to participate, however, the clinician is unlikely to accomplish anything more during the visit. Instead, this active anxiolytic intervention

Table 11.1 Step-by-step instructions for progressive muscle relaxation

Muscle group	Instructions
For each group below, every time	Instruct the patient to contract each muscle group as much as possible for 10 seconds and notice the physical sensation of the contraction. Then instruct the patient to purposefully relax for 10 seconds and notice the physical sensation of relaxation.
	Specific advice for muscle groups with the patient seated:
Toes & feet	Ask the patient to push into the floor with just their toes.
Calves	Ask the patient to push onto the balls of their feet.
Quadriceps	Ask the patient to push down into their heels.
Hamstrings	Ask the patient to draw their legs up towards their seat.
Gluteal muscles	Ask the patient to squeeze their glutes.
Abdominals	Ask the patient to contract their abdominal muscles while sitting with a straight back. Asking the patient to lean forward while contracting can help activate the muscle group.
Pectorals	Ask the patient to cross their arms.
Trapezius	Ask the patient to draw their shoulders up to their ears.
Biceps	Ask the patient to draw their hands to their shoulders.
Triceps	Ask the patient to extend their arms backward.
Forearms	Ask the patient to flex their wrists up or down.
Hands	Ask the patient to squeeze and make a fist.
	As a separate exercise, ask the patient to spread their fingers as wide as possible.
Neck	Ask the patient to draw their chin to their chest.
Face	Ask the patient to scrunch up their facial muscles.
Scalp	Ask the patient to draw their ears and eyebrows up.

treats the patient's acute anxiety and helps them later engage in sensitive discussions of difficult diagnoses, treatments, or past history. If the clinician uses a recording or computer program to play a relaxation script together, both the clinician and patient can share in a peaceful pause with minimal effort. Introducing this technique also models for the patient how behavioral coping skills are helpful outside the clinical setting.

There are many different versions of this technique. Table 11.1 provides language for helping the clinician guide the patient through relaxing different muscle groups. The clinician should describe the steps in a controlled, soothing fashion. The specific order is not important, but it feels most natural to proceed through adjacent body parts.

References

1. Conrad A, Roth WT. Muscle relaxation therapy for anxiety disorders: it works but how? *J Anxiety Disorder*. 2007;21(30):243–264.
2. Boyd JE, Lanius RA, McKinnon MC. Mindfulness-based treatments for posttraumatic stress disorder: a review of the treatment literature and neurobiological evidence. *J Psychiatry Neurosci*. 2018;43(1):7–25.

12

Use Emotional Validation to Manage Negative Countertransference

Disarm Your Negative Emotions and Humanize Your Patients

MELANIE RYLANDER, MD

Setting

In his article, *The Hateful Patient,* James Groves describes patients who instill negative emotions in clinicians.[1] With enough experience, clinicians inevitably encounter patterns of hostility, dependency, help-seeking and subsequent rejecting, and self-destruction that leave them feeling helpless, inadequate, angry, guilty, and ashamed. It becomes easy to feel disillusioned and frustrated by the apparent lack of progress among our patients.[2] Developing and maintaining resiliency requires a tool box of techniques to handle these situations. One such tool is the use of emotional validation to disarm our own negative emotions and humanize the patient.

The Technique

The first part of managing negative emotions toward a patient is to recognize them. Be mindful of your own thoughts and feelings as they arise during the encounter. Feeling hostility, aversion, inadequacy, helplessness, or even a desire to leave the room are cues that you need to self-impose an emotional intervention to continue caring for the patient. The moments when the clinician relates to the patient's experience—such as when the clinician shares the patient's feelings of helplessness—represent a perfect opportunity for emotional validation. Identify and verbalize the part of the patient's emotional experience with which you particularly relate.

Sample Dialogue

Patient: I keep coming here week after week and things never get better. I've never missed an appointment. Are you interested in helping me, or do you just care about getting paid?

Clinician: You sound frustrated about our lack of progress.

> Um, yeah. Nothing helps. Half the time I don't even think you're listening to me.

> I think in your position I'd feel the same way. It's pretty normal to feel frustrated and even angry when you feel the person who is supposed to be helping you isn't putting forth the effort. I can see why you are feeling frustrated.

> Well, it's not all your fault. I realize that.

> I'm wondering if this is a good opportunity to talk about changes we can make that might be more helpful.

Why This Works

Countertransference encompasses the clinician's emotional reactions and responses to the patient.[3] Identifying, understanding, and managing countertransference is part of any clinician's daily work and, when done properly, provides us with valuable insights about the patient. Both hateful patients and those who fail to make progress often instill negative emotions in clinicians.[1,2] This negative countertransference prevents us from seeing our patient as a human being with needs, vulnerabilities, fears, and strengths. Alienation from these qualities compromises our therapeutic relationship and clinical effectiveness.

We can re-connect with the patient by validating their emotional experience. In the sample dialogue, the clinician shares how frustrating the patient's situation is, perhaps recalling a personally experienced situation of their own or even how they feel right now with the patient. Sharing this emotion disarms the patient's hostility—and also the clinician's. Furthermore, it cultivates a collaborative relationship over an adversarial one. Finally, this technique helps clinicians share the patient's human experience. Using emotional validation with patients who are overly dependent, help seeking and rejecting, or stagnating in treatment lessens our own aversion and frustration by making the root of their struggles seem more relatable.

Identifying with someone on an emotional level leads to an increased level of intimacy between the patient and clinician. We all relate to feeling fearful, frustrated, angry, helpless, and vulnerable. Identifying how both we and our patients can simultaneously share these feelings facilitates compassion and a sense of interpersonal relatedness.

Final Thoughts

Authenticity matters. When using this technique, avoid contrived or superficial validations that can be perceived as patronizing. If you truly share the patient's emotional state, you will sound natural in saying so. But a superficial tone may induce in the patient a sense of shame or failure. Emotional validation is not the only tool used to manage negative countertransference—another approach is described in chapter 9—but this quick technique is particularly helpful when patients are angry or when you are feeling frustrated by a lack of progress in treatment. This technique lessens the clinician's own defensiveness and helps them feel increased empathy and patience in the clinical encounter.

References

1. Groves JE. Taking care of the hateful patient. *N Engl J Med.* 1978;298(16):883–887.
2. Horowitz R. Hope and expectation in the psychotherapy of the long term mentally ill. *Bull Menninger Clin.* 2008;72(4):237–258.
3. Colli A, Ferri M. Patient personality and therapist countertransference. *Curr Opin Psychiatry.* 2015;28(1):46–56.

13

Consider Fear When the Patient Is Angry
Assess What the Patient Might Be Afraid of When They Become Upset

The Setting

Unfortunately, patients are sometimes angry. Anger arises for many reasons, among them dissatisfaction with the treatment plan or disappointment with the clinician. Often patients' anger arises not from frustration with the clinician, however, as much as fear. For example, when anger is expressed in response to the treatment plan, a patient might be afraid that their concerns were not heard and are going unaddressed. When faced with an angry patient, a helpful first step is to examine what may be making the patient feel afraid.[1]

The Technique

When patients are angry, consider whether fear underlies their anger. Validate the patient's anger and ask if there is something causing them to feel afraid or uncertain. The easiest way to ask this is to be explicit: "Is there something you're afraid of?"

Sample Dialogue

Patient: I can't believe you're not changing my medications! I've been telling you over and over again how these meds aren't working, and you just aren't listening!

Clinician: You seem angry, and you feel like I haven't been listening. Is there something you're afraid of if we don't change your medications?

I'm afraid this pain is never going to go away! It's bad enough on its own but what if I'm never able to go bowling again! All I do is sit at home. It's lonely, and my friends have even invited a new person to take my spot on the team.

No wonder you want a change in medications. The pain is very difficult, you feel lonely, and you want to be active again.

Why This Works

For the clinician, dealing with angry patients can be uncomfortable at best and scary at worst. Superficially, the patient may be upset about something that happened in the appointment. The precipitant might be discussing a diagnosis, a prognosis, a medication change, or even a referral that the patient wants but the clinician does not feel is indicated. There might appear to be a perceived slight by the clinician or clinical staff such as having to wait longer than anticipated in the waiting room. Underneath this patina of anger often lies a greater, unspoken fear. The patient might be afraid that the clinician does not understand what the patient is going through or that the patient is not important to the clinician. There may be fear around what the prescription or diagnosis means for the future.

Most angry patients are not immediately aware of their fears, and their anger is an unconscious response. This technique works to resolve the patient's anger by first validating the patient's emotional state and thereby helping them de-escalate.[1] Left unspoken, fear only drives more anger whereupon the patient becomes more isolated and alienated from others. This isolation drives more fear and anger. A cycle of fear-anger-isolation ensues.

The clinician must interrupt this cycle. They do so by identifying and addressing the patient's underlying fear. This technique helps clinicians raise the question of the patient's fear and turn an angry discussion into one that is less threatening and more collaborative. Because clinicians feel more comfortable talking with scared patients than angry ones, this technique maintains a therapeutic dialogue and averts the clinician's proclivity to isolate the angry patient. In the sample dialogue, the clinician quickly recognizes the patient's anger and validates its importance and cause. The clinician then shifts to ask about what the patient fears; this shift recognizes the patient's anger as an unhealthy and unproductive response that should not itself be the focus of conversation. In shifting the conversation, the clinician gains an understanding of the patient's fears and goals. And the patient's heartfelt response is more likely to motivate the clinician to help than were the angry cajoling statements of moments earlier.

This technique reflects an approach derived from emotion-focused therapy. Emotion-focused therapy recognizes the importance of being aware of, accepting, and making sense of one's emotional experience.[2] Emotions are a vital and productive part of relationships and the human experience. However, emotional states can also be unpleasant and maladaptive. It is important to note that anger is not always maladaptive and is appropriate in certain situations. The use of this technique is recommended when the patient's anger appears to be misplaced and is interfering with the clinical relationship, the treatment, or both.

Although an open-ended question soliciting the patient's emotions might be sensible, this technique recommends a closed yes or no question. This forced choice makes it more difficult for the patient to prevaricate and easier to take ownership of a challenging emotional state.

Final Thoughts

When patients are angry, they are often primarily afraid. In validating patients' anger and considering what patients might be afraid of, clinicians can de-escalate the patient, preserve the treatment relationship, and move forward with the patient on the treatment plan. Be careful that anger does not escalate to agitation, behavioral hyperactivity, or dyscontrol. Patients who are agitated should be approached with verbal de-escalation, and clinicians should not apply the technique described in this chapter when feeling unsafe. Patients who are more escalated may better benefit from other techniques of de-escalation described elsewhere in this text (for example, chapters 8 and 16).

Reference

1. Richmond JS, Berlin JS, Fishkind AB, et al. Verbal de-escalation of the agitated patient: consensus statement of the American Association for Emergency Psychiatry Project BETA De-escalation Workgroup. *West J Emerg Med.* 2012;13(1):17–25.
2. Greenberg L. Emotion-focused therapy: a synopsis. *J Contemp Psychother.* 2006;36(2):87–93.

14

Validate the Patient's Perspective of Where They Are Now and Where They Need to Go

Understand and Support the Patient's Reality and Goals to Enhance Motivation for Treatment

Setting

Sometimes patients grow doubtful or even hopeless about treatment. These patients voice their belief that treatment is futile and improvement impossible. Patients with chronic illness may have indeed tried many treatments in the past with little success. Motivating such patients for a significant change in treatment or even a new treatment plan is difficult when the patient likely feels they have already "been there, done that" as a result of their extensive past experiences. In these situations, it is helpful for the clinician to fully validate the patient's perspective of their current health, health goals, and perceived obstacles to recharge the therapeutic relationship and build confidence in the treatment plan.

The Technique

Start with a series of questions asking the patient about their health. First, understand how the patient perceives their current health: "How do you feel about your health right now?" Validate the patient's perspective by re-phrasing the patient's statements to ensure you understand correctly. (Ideally the patient will nod or voice agreement.) Next, ask about the patient's specific goals for care: "What do you want to be different?" Again, re-state and validate these goals, eliciting a nod or statement of agreement. Then ask about the challenges the patient envisions in reaching their goals: "What do you think will get in the way of your goals?" Re-state and validate the identified obstacles and be certain the patient agrees with your summary.

Finally, and most importantly, convey to the patient that you understand their perspective and how you believe that the treatment plan will help.

Sample Dialogue

Patient: Another medication? This won't work; nothing does.

Clinician: I know you have been through a lot and tried many things to manage your diabetes. Generally, how do you feel about your health right now?

Patient: I feel like I've been sick forever, and I'll never get better.

Clinician: It sounds like you've been feeling poorly for a long time and none of the past treatments you've tried have helped. Is that right?

Sure.

What do you want to be different about your health?

Well, I don't want diabetes! At least, I want to get off insulin. I want my feet to feel better so I can start walking again.

Less insulin, less pain, and being able to walk again—is that right?

Yes!

What do you think will get in the way of these goals?

It's hard to follow my diet and take medications like I'm supposed to.

It's difficult to follow your diet and take your medications regularly. Thank you for helping me understand. I appreciate your perspective and reluctance to try something new. And, after everything we've discussed about your health, I do believe this new medication will help you. Can we talk about why I think this plan will help?

Why This Works

Patients lose hope in treatment when they fail to believe that treatment or clinicians will help. An important reason that patients lose trust in their clinicians is a sense that their clinicians do not understand them. After all, why should a patient trust a clinician who does not appreciate where their health stands, what their goals are, or what problems lie ahead? This technique helps the clinician validate the patient's perspective and generate motivation for treatment.

Validating the patient's perspective is important because it conveys to the patient that their perspective has been understood and is sensible.[1,2] This technique emphasizes the multiple elements of the patient's experience that can be validated and understood by the clinician; the clinician validates where the patient is, where they are going, and what is standing in the way. The series of questions and validating statements reinforces for the patient the value of their perspective on treatment and, just as importantly, that the clinician understands the patient's perspective. In seeking to understand and then deliberately demonstrating that you do understand, the clinician validates the patient's difficult history and the hopelessness they feel.[3] When the patient feels fully understood, they are less likely to perceive a treatment plan as just one more thing thrown at their illness by a desperate clinician but, rather, as a thoughtful and potentially helpful intervention that has been carefully considered.

In the sample dialogue, the patient feels exasperated at continued, unsuccessful treatments for diabetes. Confronted with this frustration, the clinician does not expound upon the many benefits of a new medication. Instead, the clinician deliberately validates the patient's perspective on their overall health, goals, and challenges. The clinician demonstrates to the patient an understanding of the patient's circumstances. This understanding provides the clinician credibility to say that treatment will nevertheless be helpful.

Patients who feel hopeless usually have reason to feel this way. They have been ill for a long time and have not found past treatments to be effective. They are skeptical that a new or different treatment plan—or change of clinician—will be helpful. Illness feels isolating, and the clinician's act of seeking to understand the patient's perspective ameliorates that sense of isolation and hopelessness. The isolation is replaced by an explicit partnership towards the patient's goals—a partnership in which the clinician is visibly committed towards working with the patient notwithstanding the difficult course.

Final Thoughts

On occasion, this technique leads to the clinician misunderstanding and misstating the patient's sense of their health and goals. This misunderstanding is not necessarily bad and can be clarifying for both patient and clinician. A healthy discussion to clarify the patient's perspective often ensues, which is validating for the patient and elucidating for the clinician. Ultimately, the clinician is most helpful to the patient when they fully and accurately understand the patient's perspective.

References

1. Goldstein NJ, Vezich IS, Shapiro JR. Perceived perspective taking: when others walk in our shoes. *J Pers Soc Psychol*. 2014;106(6):941–960.
2. Koerner K. *Doing Dialectical Behavior Therapy*. New York, NY: Guilford Press; 2012.
3. Lobchuk MM. Concept analysis of perspective-taking: meeting informal caregiver needs for communication competence and accurate perception. *J Adv Nurs*. 2006;54(3):330–341.

15

Share How You Feel

Put Your Own Feelings Into Words to Reset a Difficult Conversation

Setting

Many conversations in medicine are difficult. Perhaps most difficult are conversations with a hostile or angry patient who is verbally abusive—an almost universal experience in some fields.[1] Other difficult moments occur when the patient shares intense fear or anxiety. Or perhaps a sensitive memory arises during the conversation, for example, when the patient recalls an episode of abuse. Clinicians soon find themselves at a loss for words in these sensitive moments.

The Technique

When at a loss for words, explicitly share with the patient how you are feeling in that moment. To the verbally abusive patient, you might respond, "I'm feeling really scared right now." To the patient sharing a distressing memory, "I feel so sad to hear that." Do not feel pressured to follow up the statement with further questions. Let your sentiment sink into the conversation and give the patient a chance to respond.

Sample Dialogue

> Patient: I need these medications for my pain. Every day I have pain, and you have no idea what that feels like.

> Clinician: It's true, I can't know what your pain feels like. But I want to help you with your pain even if I am not going to prescribe opioids.

> You don't know what you're doing, every time I come here I get treated like trash. YOU ARE DOING A TERRIBLE JOB!

> ... Wow, I'm feeling yelled at and a little scared right now.

> ... I'm not trying to scare you, I just feel like you're not listening.

> You feel like you're not being listened to, and I want to help, but I can't do that when I don't feel safe. Let's talk about how I can help with your pain even if I cannot prescribe opioid medications.

Why This Works

This frustrating exchange demonstrates conflict between a patient who wants opioid pain medications and a clinician who does not feel comfortable prescribing them. Such conversations are increasingly frequent and necessary; fortunately, they do not typically result in such angry exchanges.[2] When confronted with a loud, angry patient, it is natural to freeze up and be uncertain what to say next. Validation may feel difficult to provide or somehow inadequate to the moment. Similarly, the clinician may feel their words to be inadequate when the patient shares unexpected emotional or sensitive information.

Interjecting with your own feelings is thus a valuable intervention for several reasons. First, it is concise. When anxious or agitated, our range of attention and cognitive abilities narrow. People can no longer attend to multiple stimuli or follow complex conversations.[3] It becomes difficult to imagine other persons' feelings and motivations. Escalated patients may fail to realize how they are being perceived. Clinicians become silent upon feeling overwhelmingly scared or sad. Pressure builds to generate a magical response that resolves the patient's problems.

Alas, no such response exists. But this technique helps de-escalate a tense situation and realize some therapeutic benefit from the moment. In this dialogue, the patient sounds angry and yells. By sharing their own emotional state, the clinician validates that the patient's experience has been heard; the clinician's expression of fear informs the patient that this escalating behavior has been noticed and evoked a response.

This technique aids the patient in mentalizing. Mentalization is the ability to understand one's own as well as other person's mental states.[4] These mental states include thoughts, feelings, and motivations. Very upset persons have difficulty mentalizing just as they have difficulty managing any complex idea or conversation. In this dialogue, the patient quickly backed off a provocative stance. Perhaps the patient was too upset to realize how they were being perceived. Or perhaps the clinician's response humanized the clinician as a person who does not deserve to be treated poorly.

Finally, this technique gives the clinician a pause to process their own intense emotional reactions. Clinical encounters are rife with charged moments, and emotional neutrality is impossible (and not ideal). Putting one's affect into words allows the clinician to recognize their own state of heart and mind—what they are feeling, what they are thinking. It is only natural to want to avoid anxiety-provoking conversations. With just a brief statement, this technique helps the clinician re-insert themselves into the shared moment with the patient. A different, more deliberative technique to managing countertransference is described in chapter 9.

The sample dialogue illustrates use of this technique in verbal de-escalation, but this approach is valuable for any emotionally laden moment. Examples in clinical encounters include a patient tearful at receiving bad news or a patient who shares their memory of a painful trauma. At these moments, the clinicians' sharing of their own feelings is a powerful act of acceptance and validation.

Final Thoughts

In this dialogue, the patient immediately backs off and re-iterates a common sentiment among frustrated patients: that they are not being heard. Afterwards, the clinician continues to validate the patient's concerns while setting immutable limits around prescribing. Sometimes, when this technique is used in verbal de-escalation, patients feel ashamed or embarrassed. The clinician should validate these responses. The patient may apologize, and the clinician should only accept that apology if they feel they genuinely can. Otherwise, continue to validate and move on with the business of the encounter.

References

1. Khademloo M, Moonesi FS, Gholizade H. Health care violence and abuse towards nurses in hospitals in north of Iran. *Glob J Health Sci.* 2013;5(4):211–216.
2. Pourmand A, Jasani G, Shay C, Mazer-Amirshahi M. The evolving landscape of acute pain management in the era of the opioid crisis. *Curr Pain Headache Rep.* 2018;22(11):73.
3. Easterbrook JA. The effect of emotion on cue utilization and the organization of behavior. *Psychol Rev.* 1959;66(3):183–201.
4. Bateman A, Fonagy P. *Psychotherapy for Borderline Personality Disorder: Mentalization-based Treatment.* New York, NY: Oxford University Press; 2004.

16

Agree to Disagree

De-Escalate an Argument by Repeating This Short Phrase

Setting

Try as we might to work through difficult conversations, validate opposing viewpoints, assuage differences, and find common ground with our patients, sometimes we simply disagree. These disagreements are sometimes very dramatic—consider the patient who wants but lacks capacity to discharge from the hospital—or smaller yet poignant encounters in the office setting. Perhaps the clinician is frustrated that validation has not helped the patient feel better, or perhaps the conversation is escalating to include yelling or visible signs of agitation. Clinicians can acknowledge a difference of opinion and reinforce limits.

The Technique

Use the short phrase, "We have to agree to disagree," in situations where disagreement is unavoidable. Patients who are agitated may need to hear this line several times. After reiterating this phrase, the clinician may progress to other questions or choices for the patient in order to continue verbal de-escalation or other business of the clinical encounter.

Sample Dialogue

Patient: I need to leave the hospital; you can't make me stay here.

Clinician: I'm sorry, you can't leave right now. You have an IV in place, and we are worried that you are not thinking clearly.

I...don't need here!

Well, we just have to agree to disagree. You cannot leave right now.

> You can't keep here me. This isn't jail, I have to leave! Leave!

> We just have to agree to disagree. You cannot leave right now. I will do everything I can to help you feel more comfortable while you are here. Maybe I can get you some water?

Why This Works

Disagreements happen. These exchanges frustrate both patients and clinicians: patients do not want to be sick, clinicians do not want to disappoint patients and often feel as though they have failed. Nevertheless, the clinician's duty is to the patient's health and safety rather than their feelings. In the sample dialogue, a patient who is apparently confused (and making misstatements) wants to leave the hospital. The clinician notes that the patient has intravenous lines in place and is not thinking clearly. If this patient cannot leave, there is no room for compromise on that point. When other de-escalation strategies like validation and offering choices are insufficient, the clinician needs a new de-escalation strategy.

"Agree to disagree" is a helpful phrase for these situations.[1] Upset or confused patients have difficulty following complex statements and instructions. This phrase is short, easy to say, and easy to understand. The phrase also works because validation is the cornerstone of verbal de-escalation, and the clinician begins with a validating notion—that the clinician and patient agree on something. Still, clear limits are set. The idea that there is disagreement is made explicitly clear, and the patient is not given a choice on the most critical decision at hand. Being explicit is helpful for both parties; ambiguity can further frustrate the agitated patient.

Finally, that this statement is so easy to say endows the clinician with confidence in setting limits. Many clinicians have difficulty laying down the law when necessary—they entered a healing profession and seek collaborative relationships with patients. Yet patients in unsafe or difficult circumstances require firm limits for their own safety. It is not an exaggeration to say that agitated or impaired patients may depend on such firm limits for their lives. Even in outpatient settings, overly permissive practices such as overprescribing of opioids have proven deadly.[2] By asserting that, "We must agree to disagree"—and repeating it if necessary—the clinician reinforces their own confidence in setting clear limits. The clinician's goal in these encounters is to speak with authority without being authoritarian.[3]

This technique closes the door on one part of the conversation (here, whether or not the patient may leave) but opens the door for collaboration in other areas. In the sample dialogue, the clinician begins exploring what the patient might find helpful for calming himself given that he cannot leave the hospital.

Final Thoughts

Clinician-patient relationships are formed in a crucible of illness and stress. The clinician's responsibility is to provide their expertise in the patient's interest, and in so doing conflict may become unavoidable. Resolving conflict and de-escalating an agitated patient is a skill that requires multiple approaches and trial-and-error by the clinician. This technique and simple phrase help the clinician assert limits in a validating, compassionate, and firm manner.

References

1. Richmond JS, Berlin JS, Fishkind AB, et al. Verbal de-escalation of the agitated patient: consensus statement of the American Association for Emergency Psychiatry Project BETA De-escalation Workgroup. *West J Emerg Med*. 2012;13(1):17–25.
2. Makary MA, Overton HN, Wang P. Overprescribing is major contributor to opioid crisis. *BMJ*. 2017;359:j4792.
3. Berlin J. Collaborative de-escalation. In: Zeller SL, Nordstrom K, Wilson MP, eds. *The Diagnosis and Management of Agitation*. Cambridge, UK: Cambridge University Press; 2017.

17

Be Honest About Your Limitations
Relieve Yourself of Unobtainable Expectations and Reset the Conflictual Encounter

Setting

Sometimes clinicians cannot deliver what patients want or need. There may be disagreement over a diagnosis or use of a certain treatment, or maybe the patient wants something that the clinician feels they cannot provide. Most clinicians enter the field in order to learn and deliver life-saving treatments, and it is natural to feel frustrated when good options are unavailable. Clinicians are understandably hurt by upset patients' statements that speak to our own shortcomings—patients who state, "You don't know what you're doing," or "If you mess this up, I'll sue you."

The Technique

When challenged with lawsuits or on your own competence, be honest about your own limitations. A great phrase for framing this discussion is, "I can only do my best." When the patient is agitated or upset, repeat this phrase as a de-escalation tactic. Once the clinician is frank about their own limitations, the discussion may turn to the more limited set of available choices or treatments.

Sample Dialogue

Patient: My blood sugars are out of control. I read online about all these people whose diabetes is cured with a medication or two. What's going on?

Clinician: I wish your sugars were better, too. I have a few ideas that we can...

Ideas? Your ideas don't work! Do you even know what you're doing?

I hear that you're frustrated. I can only do my best, and I'll help you as best I can.

Your best? Puh-lease!

I can only do my best. I know you're frustrated. There are still some options we should discuss, if you're willing.

OK, let's hear your ideas.

Why This Works

Even experienced clinicians have difficulty hearing statements like those in the dialogue. Most clinicians' first response may not even be to feel angry or upset but rather to feel themselves incapable. This reaction can be explained in terms of projective identification. Projective identification (PI) can be experienced by clinicians working with patients who employ the primitive defense mechanism of projection.[1] Projection occurs when a patient is unable to tolerate highly negative feelings (e.g., self-hatred or anger) and, rather than accepting these feeling as their own, believes that it is the clinician who is experiencing those feelings. For example, if the patient is feeling self-hatred, the patient instead thinks, "the clinician hates me." If the clinician then begins to feel and behave with dislike toward the patient, the clinician is experiencing PI. The patient's negative projection is hence reinforced. Clearly, PI becomes problematic for the treatment alliance.

PI occurs when working among patients with more severe psychopathology who use primitive defenses like projection, but everyone uses unsophisticated coping skills when distressed and overwhelmed. The clinician should always be aware of their feelings towards the patient. This sample patient is frustrated at being unable to control their hyperglycemia; the frustration is made worse by the perception that other people's diabetes is being cured while theirs is not. What an incredibly scary, frustrating situation! The clinician appropriately validates the patient's emotional state and offers additional treatment options. But the patient still feels upset.

The clinician responds, "I can only do my best." This succinct statement humanizes the clinician and acknowledges the present limitations. In the above dialogue, the clinician probably shares the patient's frustrations over their blood sugars. This phrase conveys this sense that the patient and clinician are in a difficult situation together. Recognizing the collaborative aspect of the treatment relationship is important. The clinician may already have been partly (even inadvertently) blaming the patient for hyperglycemia due to their non-adherence with diet, exercise, or medication recommendations.[2]

Finally, the phrase acts as a soothing mantra for the clinician, a self-directed reminder that they are both doing the best job they can with a difficult illness. The clinician and patient are together grappling with shortcomings of available treatments in the face of an unrelenting chronic disease. The clinician in this example might go on to share their own frustration with the limitations of available treatments and the adherence challenges they pose.

This proposed phrasing may sound somewhat peculiar at first. Why not say, "I am doing my best?" There are several reasons that, "I can only do my best," works better. Coming from most people—the authors included—the former phrase has a whining tone reminiscent of a schoolyard failure. The clinician wants to assert confidence, starting with the statement, "I can." At the same time, this technique acknowledges the patient's sense of limitation by including the word, "only." It is thus both a more confident and also a more validating statement. Another reason this phrasing works is that it is more likely to be true: every clinician has off days in which they are feeling less patient, less clever, or more burned out. Encounters like in the sample dialogue do not help. Some days, the clinician is not at their best. The latter phrase can be stated with confidence at any time. It is always important and more effective to be authentic.

Final Thoughts

Clinicians may feel incapable when confronted with these accusatory statements of incompetence, but another common feeling is to be left speechless and disarmed. This technique is good for intense moments when one needs to regain composure and think about next steps in the interview. Validation is an essential part of the clinician's toolkit for helping the patient but also for re-gaining one's own composure. This technique reminds the clinician that they need not identify with the ineffective role being projected upon them by the frustrated patient.

As the patient de-escalates, they will often apologize that they were not speaking in a productive or kind manner previously. Whether to accept the apology is a personal choice by the clinician. But all clinicians should feel comfortable in thanking the patient for being thoughtful, validating the difficulty of the present situation, and moving on to treatment planning.

References

1. Corradi RB. The psychodynamics of borderline psychopathology. *Bull Menninger Clin.* 2015;79(3):203–231.
2. Carr AJ, Donovan JL. Why doctors and patients disagree. *Br J Rheumatol.* 1998;37(1):1–4.

II
Taking a History

18

Be Curious

When Curious About What a Patient Has Said, Ask More Questions to Obtain Useful Information and Show the Patient That You Are Interested

RACHEL GLICK, MD

Setting

In a world of electronic medical records and evidence-based medicine, clinicians are quick to rely on existing documentation for the patient's story. In many hospital charts, there are notes from a variety of physicians, nurses, social workers, students, and others. It may seem like a time-saver to forgo asking the patient questions that are already documented. Yet this shortcut leads clinicians to miss important facts about the patient and lose the opportunity to connect with the patient through a more complete understanding of their story. Spending a little extra time to review with the patient the history that has been codified in their record can add a richness to your interactions and give you valuable information that you would not otherwise obtain.

The Technique

Never assume that the medical record supplies the entire story. After looking at the history in the patient's medical record, ask the patient to tell you their story directly. Be curious and ask the questions that come to your mind as the patient shares their history with you. These questions do not need to relate to the chief complaint or initial presentation. Sometimes clarification of what may seem like a small point opens a world of deeper understanding.

Sample Dialogue

Patient: I'm sorry to be here again, doc. I feel okay, but I see how everybody here looks at me in this ER and thinks "not him again."

Clinician: Why do you think that?

I come in here over and over. You finally talked me into detox and rehab and I did really good and was sober for 5 months, but here I am again. I started drinking again on Saturday after seeing my daughter.

I saw in your chart that you have a daughter, but there were not many details. Tell me about her.

She's grown now, but I really want to have a relationship with her again. My being a drunk gets in the way.

What happened to your relationship?

When my wife died, Rosie was only 2 years old, and I started drinking so her grandmother took her. And I just kept drinking since there was no reason to stop.

I didn't even realize you had been married. I'm sorry to hear that your wife died. Did you see Rosie at all as she was growing up?

My mother-in-law let me visit a few times early on, but I was always drinking and I was embarrassed to see Rosie when I was drunk, so I stopped visiting. Then I finally got sober, so I called Rosie and we met. It was real nice, but afterword I stopped at the party store and got a couple of bottles and now I am back here. Rosie looks just like her mom…so pretty…and I miss her mom so much.

Why This Works

Everyone has a story and an experience of life that is not immediately visible to others. Sonder (a contemporary neologism) describes the realization that others have emotional stories as rich as our own yet unknown to us.[1,2] The idea of sonder allows the possibility of infinite curiosity about others' inner-lives. As clinicians we have the privilege of being allowed to ask about others' emotional experiences in the course of our work. Sonder, perhaps from the words "special" and "wonder," is a powerful tool for the clinical interview.

Exhibiting sonder and asking questions with curiosity allows the patient to share their story and thereby affirms the worth of that story. It is easy for clinicians in busy primary care and emergency settings to spend very little time talking about issues that seem to be buried in the past. But this dialogue exemplifies how much detail and nuance can go undocumented in the chart. Here, the clinician gains an understanding of the significance of the patient's wife's death in relation to his drinking behavior. The patient's motivations are clearer, and the clinician is in a better position to support the patient's efforts to stop drinking. In just a minute the interviewer uncovers an entire social history that was either never obtained or lost among the patient's old records. The interviewer makes a connection with a frequently seen patient in a way perhaps no one ever had before.

In her essay, "Curiosity," Dr. Faith Fitzgerald writes how curiosity in medicine is increasingly threatened by the emphasis on examinable facts, the focus on efficiency in our hospitals and clinics, and our reliance on technology.[3] Yet sonder and the curiosity that naturally arises from it enrich the patient's care. Curiosity makes our relationships with patients more interesting and lively. For the clinician, curiosity lies at the heart of our desire to understand the patient's problems and emotional responses. This understanding helps us treat the specific needs of the individual patient. In this example, understanding that the patient—who may be dismissed by some as "single" or "alcoholic"—is also a grieving husband and father opens a new level of understanding and compassion in the therapeutic relationship.

Final Thoughts

Questioning a patient with curiosity helps the interviewer learn new information even about the patient who may be considered well known. This technique is especially helpful for patients who return again and again without appreciable improvement. Asking about a past history that is presumably well documented in past records might lead some patients to tell you that the information you are asking for is already in their record. Patients may also react negatively if they feel that the clinician's questioning is voyeuristic. However, these reactions are rare when the clinician approaches this topic from a genuine and validating position. More often patients are happy to answer probing questions when they are asked with kindness and curiosity. These questions allow you to see your patient in a new way.

References

1. Bowman D. On sonder. *Med Humanities*. 2015;41(2):75–76.
2. Rosenberg AR. Escaping sonder. *J Pain Symptom Manage*. 2018;56(3):e1–e2.
3. Fitzgerald FT. Curiosity. *Ann Intern Med*. 1999;130(1):70–72.

19

Prioritize Information You Need Right Now

Shift Your Line of Questioning Without Shifting the Topic

DAVID KROLL, MD

Setting

Some lines of questions naturally evoke discomfort and opposition. Patients' resistance to speaking about certain topics may be overt (e.g., they argue), but oftentimes it is more subtle: patients grow quiet, deflect questions, or display negative emotions. Although circumstances exist in which it is medically necessary to continue soliciting sensitive information regardless of whether it upsets the patient, insisting on answers from the uncomfortable patient is more often counterproductive. Prioritizing the specific information you need right now builds a working relationship in a less provocative—and more productive—way.

The Technique

Notice how the patient responds to a potentially sensitive question, and consider how essential obtaining a complete answer to that exact question is for the patient's care. Prioritize your line of questioning to target the information you know that you need now, without entirely shifting the topic. If a patient discloses a recent trauma, for example, you probably need to know what kinds of injuries were sustained and whether any physical or behavioral symptoms are present that require treatment. However, you likely do not need to press the patient for other details that do not directly and immediately inform your assessment or treatment plan.

Sample Dialogue

Clinician: That bruise looks painful, what happened?

Patient: I was assaulted.

> I'm so sorry. Tell me what happened.

> Well, um, I don't know. It was late…we were all drinking…um…

> You know, I see how upset you are. I actually don't need to hear all the details right now. My first priority is making sure you are safe. Where have you been hurt?

> Just here, over my eye.

> Did you lose consciousness at any point?

Why This Works

Soliciting information from a patient is a negotiation. Patients are ultimately in control of what they share regarding their personal health, and they share it on the premise that doing so enables clinicians to take better care of them.[1] Patients will not automatically appreciate the benefit of sharing all the information they have in all cases, and clinicians do not have the authority to demand that information. Clinicians are more successful in soliciting a history when the need for information is readily apparent and the patient feels safe answering.

Attending to the patient's feelings in the context of an encounter is critical for developing a strong rapport which in turn is essential for achieving the best possible clinical outcome.[2] Demonstrating sensitivity to a patient's reactions, whether spoken or unspoken, engenders trust in the clinician and fosters a treatment environment that feels safe. Over time, topics that initially provoke discomfort become easier to broach.

This sample dialogue demonstrates a challenging interaction with a patient who was recently traumatized. In cases of recent trauma, prying into details when the patient feels uncomfortable can cause iatrogenic harm.[3] Many years ago, the prevailing notion was that individuals should undergo a psychological debriefing after a traumatic event in which the event is recounted. This approach has since been associated with an increased risk of developing post-traumatic stress disorder and is now discouraged.[3] Questions that align with the patient's immediate goals in coming to see you will more readily be answered; for example, to address injuries or assist with a referral to social, legal, or mental health services. This conversation can be used as a starting point for a broader clinical interaction. As you accumulate information on ostensibly more neutral topics, you will inevitably clarify additional history. This discussion also establishes the rapport required to advance treatment.

This technique does not exempt clinicians or patients from discussing uncomfortable topics when it is medically necessary to do so. For instance, when substance abuse is impacting a patient's health, ignoring the subject is not appropriate. Instead, a patient's resistance to engaging around this topic should re-direct the clinical interview to be less confrontational.[4] If "Are you a heavy drinker?" elicits a negative response, try "How many days per week do you usually drink alcohol?" which does not convey judgment or impart the pejorative label of "drinker."

Final Thoughts

When in doubt, let the patient guide you as to how to best approach a topic. However, be careful not to assume that certain topics make patients feel uncomfortable just because you expect them to be sensitive or because you do not know how to ask about them. For example, many clinicians are reluctant to ask patients from sexual minority groups about their sexual health even though this information is important to gather. Moreover, avoiding the subject only reinforces this group's marginalization in healthcare.[5] Instead convey that you are comfortable asking and hearing about sensitive material whenever and however the patient chooses to share it.

References

1. Gafni A, Charles C, Whelan T. The physician-patient encounter: the physician as a perfect agent for the patient versus the informed treatment decision-making model. *Soc Sci Med.* 1998;47(3):347–354.
2. Ferguson WJ, Candib LM. Culture, language, and the doctor-patient relationship. *Fam Med.* 2002;34(5):353–361.
3. Kearns MC, Ressler KJ, Zatzick D, Rothbaum BO. Early interventions for PTSD: a review. *Depress Anxiety.* 2012;29(10):833–842.
4. Miller WR. Motivational interviewing: research, practice, and puzzles. *Addict Behav.* 1996;21(6):835–842.
5. Makodon HJ. Ending LGBT invisibility in health care: the first step in ensuring equitable care. *Cleve Clin J Med.* 2011;78(4):220–224.

20
Use Open-Ended Questions
for Sensitive Topics
Invite Greater Honesty and Avoid a Sense of Judgment Through Open-Ended Questions

Setting

Patients may be reluctant to disclose sensitive information. This reluctance may stem from embarrassment, fear of consequences, or a sense that the information is not relevant to the clinical interview. A skilled interviewer helps the patient feel at ease and comfortable in discussing difficult topics including those related to sex, substance abuse, and personal relationships that directly affect health and treatment planning.

The Technique

Utilize open-ended questions when approaching sensitive topics. Closed questions ask for the patient to answer "yes" or "no." Rather than limiting the range of possible responses before the patient even answers, ask open-ended questions that begin with "How often," "How come," or "When." Open-ended questions can be particularly helpful for elaborating upon particular symptoms.

Sample Dialogue

Patient: I do notice that my headaches seem to be worse when I have a beer.

Clinician: How often do you drink alcohol?

About as often as most people, I guess.

Ah, ok. So in a typical week, how many days would you say you drink?

A drink or two after dinner, more on the weekends.

Why This Works

Open-ended questions are useful at almost any point of the clinical encounter. Most visits start with such questions—"What brings you in today?"—but the fast pace of encounters may lead clinicians to start using closed questions during the interview to purportedly be more efficient and targeted. Yet oftentimes this practice leads to a less reliable history and poorer therapeutic relationships without shortening the interview.

Clinicians' use of open-ended questions is associated with a stronger therapeutic relationship.[1] An open-ended question allows the patient to respond in an unconstrained manner befitting their conversational style. It also allows the clinician to maintain a neutral, non-judgmental stance. Many patients infer a right or wrong, better or worse answer based on how the clinician phrases a question. The clinician-patient relationship should not include pressure to answer questions in a certain way. The implications of avoiding such guiding questions are significant: the clinician's perceived empathy and communication quality is among the most important correlates with the patient's sense of satisfaction with the clinical encounter.[1-3]

The utility of open-ended interview questions is recognized in many psychotherapy models and especially emphasized in motivational interviewing.[4] Open-ended interviewing facilitates the development of clinical rapport and a better understanding of the patient's history and thinking. In the above example, the patient betrays a sense that while they may drink most days, they do not feel this amount to be excessive. It would not be surprising to find that the patient's family or friends drink similarly. These would be essential considerations in any conversation about problematic use.

Relationship-building is not the only reason to utilize this technique frequently. Allowing a freer response also invites a more accurate answer. In the sample dialogue, imagine how the patient might have been pressured to respond if the clinician asked, "Do you have more than two drinks per day?" (The definition of at-risk drinking for men.)[5] A patient might suspect troubling implications of an affirmative answer. Even more concerning would be the patient who has a significant alcohol problem that is missed but may have been caught incidentally as part of an open-ended exchange. The value of open-ended questions in obtaining an accurate account of substance use is reflected in its application in standardized screeners for substance use disorders.[6] Moreover, the use of this technique need not result in a longer interview. In the above, the patient's response took barely a moment longer than a simple yes or no while being significantly more helpful.

Final Thoughts

An interview is not simply an exchange of information between the clinician and patient; it is a collaborative process of building a therapeutic alliance and using that alliance to solve problems. Open-ended questions are not only for the beginning of the interview but should be used liberally throughout the encounter. Table 20.1 demonstrates how some common closed questions may be asked in an open-ended fashion. Of course, close-ended questions may be necessary—for instance, in asking about the pertinent absence of particular symptoms.

Table 20.1 Re-phrasing closed questions as open-ended

Closed question	Open-ended question
Are you here today to discuss your pain?	What is the most important thing we need to discuss today?
Do you have any allergies?	What allergies do you have to medications or food?
Do you smoke?	How often do you smoke?
Are you having pain?	Tell me about any pain you are having.
Do you take any other medications?	What other medications do you take?
Is there anything else you want to discuss?	What else would you like to discuss before we finish?

References

1. Mikesell L. Medicinal relationships: caring conversation. *Med Educ.* 2013;47(5):443–452.
2. Welch SJ. Twenty years of patient satisfaction research applied to the emergency department: a qualitative review. *Am J Med Qual.* 2010;25(1):64–72.
3. Vukmir RB. Customer satisfaction with patient care: "where's the beef?". *J Hosp Mark Public Relations.* 2006;17(1):79–107.
4. Center for Substance Abuse Treatment. *Enhancing Motivation for Change in Substance Abuse Treatment.* Rockville, MD: Substance Abuse and Mental Health Services Administration; 1999.
5. National Institute on Alcohol Abuse and Alcoholism. *Helping Patients Who Drink Too Much: A Clinician's Guide.* Washington, DC: U.S. Department of Health and Human Services; 2005.
6. National Institute on Drug Abuse. *The NIDA Quick Screen;* 2012. Accessed online December 21, 2018: www.drugabuse.gov/publications/resource-guide-screening-drug-use-in-general-medical-settings/nida-quick-screen.

21

Attend to Affect

Emphasize the Patient's Emotional Words for a Richer History

Setting

Clinicians need to obtain a lot of information during the patient encounter. Unfortunately, collecting all this data sometimes feels like a chore as both the clinician and patient run through a checklist of symptoms. It is also easy to miss important information that does not fit neatly into the checklist. These interviews grow lifeless for the patient and boring for the clinician. One must strike a balance between the patient's spontaneous history and a necessary, thorough collection of data.

The Technique

Attend to the patient's affect and emotional words. Affect is the patient's portrayal of emotion, whether through nonverbal cues or emotional words. Emotional words are those that a patient uses to describe how they are feeling. These words are often easy to identify, for example, "sad," "angry," "scared." Other emotional words might be more nuanced: "frustrated," "fail," or "looking forward to." Repeat the emotional word back to the patient and invite elaboration. In the case of a nonverbal cue, describe the emotion that you are seeing—perhaps, "you look worried"—and let the patient respond with their own emotional word.

Sample Dialogue

Clinician: When did your headaches start?

Patient: About a week ago

What makes them worse?

It's worse during the day. Sometimes I used a heating pad but then got scared. Then when I'm on my feet for a while the pain is worse.

Scared? How come scared?

I would put the heating pad on, but I would feel dizzy and light-headed. Recently I have these episodes where I feel kind of weak in my knees, my heart starts racing, and my chest feels tight. That's when my headaches happen.

Why This Works

Emphasizing emotional words is important during the interview. First, this technique helps build rapport with the patient. Neurologically, humans are built to form relationships based on emotional cues.[1] Introducing an emotional context to the interview generates a more open, comfortable relationship in which the patient feels invited to disclose their history. This tendency towards emotional relationships also readies the patient to receive clinical advice. The patient finds the clinician's exploration of emotions comforting, and in turn the patient responds with trust and a willingness to accept treatment recommendations. Regardless of the setting, a successful relationship is predicated on the idea that another person is perceptive to our emotional states.[2] By talking about feelings, a clinical interview that had risked becoming monotonous can become a more interesting, rewarding partnership between patient and clinician.

Another reason that this technique works relates to how our brains process memories. The neuroanatomical structures related to emotional processing are intricately involved in memory formation.[3] Emotions are part of our stories. In the clinical encounter, helping the patient access the emotional context for a memory helps them retrieve richer, more detailed memories. In this sample dialogue, chasing the patient's expression of fear led to a more helpful history—as well as some concerning additional symptoms that could have been missed.

When they occur, portrayals of affect and emotional words are clinical cues for deeper content. When a patient decides to seek care, some part of them is readying to share what is bothering them. But just as it is human nature to form emotional bonds, we also seek to avoid anxiety. Some patients find comfort in a "checklist-y" interview that is highly structured, because it is less likely to reveal anxiety-provoking content. Indeed, clinicians too find comfort in the routine of a symptom checklist. However, a stronger patient relationship built on emotional content makes it easier and quicker to gather an accurate history. This relationship will later yield a stronger alliance in planning treatment.

Some patients have a hard time holding back once emotions are introduced into the conversation. Some patients proceed to reveal significant anxiety, mood symptoms, prior trauma, deeply seeded regrets, or suicidal thoughts. Clinicians quickly fret that they have opened a Pandora's Box of new problems. In fact, these uncovered problems are probably the most important issues related to the patient's encounter. And having validated the patient by chasing their affect, the clinician is well-positioned to be a therapeutic support. Other techniques are described in this text for helping patients manage intense affect (for example, chapters 6, 8, and 15).

Final Thoughts

Shy or embarrassed patients who are reluctant to talk often respond well to this technique, and the clinician might apply this technique when feeling stuck with a patient who does not talk much.

This technique offers the clinician a way to respond to the patient's nonverbal communication. One pitfall of responding to nonverbal cues is empathic failure in which the clinician offers an emotional word that does not fit the patient's experience. Most patients will simply correct the clinician, but others may feel invalidated or upset. The clinician's response in such cases is simple: invite the patient to describe how they are feeling and begin again. When really at a loss to describe the affect behind a nonverbal cue, share your puzzlement as a starting point for discussion: "I noticed that your expression changed, as if you are feeling something. How are you feeling now?"

References

1. Butler EA. Emotions are temporal interpersonal systems. *Curr Opin Psychol.* 2017;17:129–134.
2. Wiebe SA, Johnson SM. Creating relationships that foster resilience in emotionally focused therapy. *Curr Opin Psychol.* 2017;13:65–69.
3. Riegel M, Wierzba M, Grabowska A, Jednorog K, Marchewka A. Effect of emotion on memory for words and their context. *J Comp Neurol.* 2016;524(8):1636–1645.

22
Validate and Move
Use Validation as a Transitional Tool in the Unwieldy Interview

Setting

A diagnostic interview requires clinicians to collect a lot of information with little time. Trainees and even experienced practitioners often struggle to reign in tangential and over-inclusive patients. Digressive or talkative patients do not always provide information essential to diagnosis and treatment planning. Good interviewers need to be able to pivot from non-essential topics without frustrating the patient.

The Technique

If the patient is digressing, interrupt them kindly with a validating statement. After you have validated, reframe the interview towards a more productive topic.

Sample Dialogue

Patient: ...but then it's impossible to take my depression medications because the kids get me off track. I'll be up in the morning trying to get things done and my son just doesn't want to sleep. I don't know if you have kids, but when they don't sleep at night and get up early...

Clinician: Sounds like it's been difficult for you to take medications regularly. How is your mood affecting you at work?

Work has actually been going ok. We have a few big projects underway, and I've been able to keep up with my job.

Why This Works

Although many clinicians worry about upsetting patients by cutting them off, an efficient use of time and valid assessment will be far more valuable to the patient. Most patients rarely mind their clinician re-directing the conversation. What might feel rude in social settings is appropriate within the frame of a patient encounter. Patients trust their clinician to guide a diagnostic and therapeutic interview. Trainees in particular are often far more worried about interrupting patients than patients are about being interrupted.

Nonetheless, one must avoid peppering the patient with questions lest an interview start to feel like an interrogation. Many patients with a history of trauma or anxiety are prone to a sense of invalidation and fear others' attempt to control the clinical interaction. The clinician can ameliorate these fears by interjecting with a validating statement. There are many ways to validate: you can agree with the facts of a statement (as in the above exchange), you can agree with how the patient is feeling, or you can use some of the other strategies described in this text.[1] It is harder for the patient to begrudge a supportive statement then an outright redirection of the interview. And validating statements have the not inconsequential ancillary benefit of improving the quality of care.[2]

Once the interviewer again has the stage, there is an opportunity to pivot to a topic of choice. In fact, the clinician can make a fairly big leap in interview if necessary. In this exchange, the clinician asks about a barely related topic without the conversation losing its flow. This ability to move is helpful when the clinician forgets to ask something in the interview and remembers later.

This validate-and-move technique is easily combined with other interviewing skills in this text. Indeed, it is never bad to reassure the patient that you are listening closely and trying to understand their experience. The therapeutic alliance represents one of the clinicians' strongest therapeutic tools; strengthening that alliance pays dividends in effectiveness and efficiency.

If you realize early on that the patient will need some direction for the interview, consider providing a series of early validating statements without a pivot. For example, interrupt by validating, then let the patient continue. These brief interjections serve several purposes. They build rapport with the patient early in order to ease later, more directed conversation. The patient grows accustomed to positive, non-judgmental interruptions. And even these mild re-directions help the clinician assess the patient's mental status—Do they maintain the same train of thought, or do their thoughts derail? Impairments in thought process, memory, or attention may be revealed by the interviewer's complicating the interaction, however mildly.

Final Thoughts

Often talkative patients are trying to be helpful by providing lots of information. There are certainly pearls to be found in these histories, and many clinicians are prone to cutting off patients far too soon—one study found the physicians typically interrupt their patients after about 11 seconds.[3] But there also comes a time when the clinician has to help the patient by prioritizing elements of the interview, thereby aiding the patient to take advantage of their knowledge and experience.

References

1. Richmond JS, Berlin JS, Fishkind AB, et al. Verbal de-escalation of the agitated patient: consensus statement of the American Association for Emergency Psychiatry Project BETA De-escalation Workgroup. *West J Emerg Med.* 2012;13(1):17–25.
2. Epstein RM, Shields CG, Franks P, Meldrum SC, Feldman M, Kravitz RL. Exploring and validating patient concerns: relation to prescribing for depression. *Ann Fam Med.* 2007;5(1):21–28.
3. Singh Ospina N, Phillips KA, Rodriguez-Gutierrez R, et al. Eliciting the patient's agenda-secondary analysis of recorded clinical encounters. *J Gen Intern Med.* 2018;34(1):36–40.

23

Write a Timeline

Organize Chaotic Histories and Validate the Patient's Experience

Setting

Not all patients present an organized and detailed account of their illness. Anxiety, memory impairment, a sense of feeling overwhelmed—all contribute to patients' inability to share their own stories. Obtaining a history may be particularly challenging for patients with more severe pathology including thought process or personality disorders. Other patients present with a variety of social stressors of unclear (but suspiciously significant) relevance to their visit.

The Technique

When struggling to ascertain the patient's history of present illness, write a timeline together with the patient. The most recent event—the encounter—goes on the far right. Then work with the patient to fill in relevant events that led up to the visit. Important recent events (e.g., first onset of symptoms, loss of employment) can be used as anchors around which more specific details are added. For emergent presentations, work backwards step-by-step over events that led to the patient's decision to seek treatment. The clinician should write the timeline and freely incorporate events that the patient feels are important; information deemed extraneous can be disregarded later. Figure 23.1 illustrates a timeline generated after the sample dialogue.

Sample Dialogue

> Patient: I need help with this pain. I'm hurting all over and can't do anything that I need to do. Before I was doing ok but not great, then things started happening and the pain wouldn't let me keep up…

> Clinician: Wow, sounds like there is a lot going on. It would help me if we can write down some of this to get a sense of your symptoms. Is it okay if we do this together?

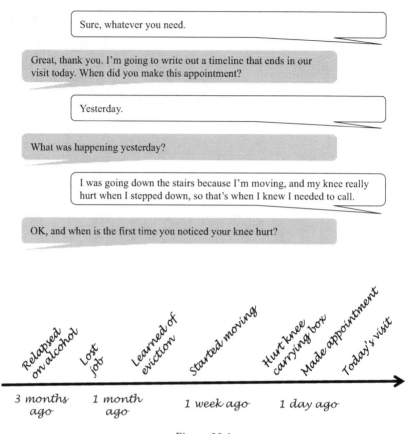

> Sure, whatever you need.

> Great, thank you. I'm going to write out a timeline that ends in our visit today. When did you make this appointment?

> Yesterday.

> What was happening yesterday?

> I was going down the stairs because I'm moving, and my knee really hurt when I stepped down, so that's when I knew I needed to call.

> OK, and when is the first time you noticed your knee hurt?

Relapsed on alcohol · Lost job · Learned of eviction · Started moving · Hurt knee carrying box · Made appointment · Today's visit

3 months ago | 1 month ago | 1 week ago | 1 day ago

Figure 23.1

Why This Works

Under the best of circumstances, it is difficult to recall the timing, details, exacerbating and ameliorating events, and motivations of physical and psychiatric symptoms. Eliciting this history from an anxious or disorganized patient is challenging. Even worse, the patient's difficulty in presenting a history generates impatience and frustration in the clinician who is in a hurry and under pressure to offer a solution for what may be an obscure diagnosis.

Writing a timeline is easy and natural. Humans are neurologically predisposed to order events chronologically in a linear fashion.[1] When used in a clinical interview, a timeline helps both the patient and clinician to organize the history of present illness and recover details of the presentation that may have been lost in a less orderly retelling. A timeline helps relate the appearance of symptoms to significant life events. Perhaps a significant social stressor like the loss of a loved one or job plays into the patient's visit. These events are difficult to incorporate into a traditional medical history but may play a significant role in how illness presents and is managed. A timeline incorporates disparate events into a clear sequence. When available, information from collateral informants may also contribute to a detailed timeline.

This technique is also of benefit as a form of validation. Writing the patient's words is a straightforward form of validation—the patient becomes aware that their story matters and is being heard. The clinician is given multiple opportunities to reflect and clarify the patient's experience through completing the timeline. In addition, seeing their written history reduces the patient's fear that something important will go unregarded.

By engaging both the clinician and patient in the shared task of understanding the presentation, writing a timeline enhances the therapeutic relationship. The clinician is freed from the pressure to become an organizing influence on the patient's chaotic storytelling. And the patient is satisfied to be able to meet the clinician's needs in a straightforward, easily observed manner. Writing a timeline results in a tangible product for the patient and clinician to use in formulating a diagnosis and planning treatment.

The timeline thus carries therapeutic value (by validating the patient's story) as well as diagnostic value (in organizing the history). The timeline technique is utilized in several therapeutic models including cognitive behavior and crisis intervention therapies.[2]

Figure 23.1 shows a timeline that was produced by the clinician and patient from the sample dialogue. There are some typical descriptions of the pain that a clinician would ask for in a typical history. However, there are also some significant life events that preceded the visit including loss of a job and relapse on alcohol. The relationship among these events and the patient's visit merits further exploration, as these are clearly issues that will impact the patient's recovery. The timeline illustrates how this technique can save time in the appointment. Loss of employment is a very stressful life event and recounting that event might consume a clinical interview; here, the clinician may quickly validate the patient's experience by including it on the timeline but only decide later whether to pursue more details or focus elsewhere. The event's occurrence is recorded and easily re-accessed at a later time for more discussion.

Final Thoughts

This technique is helpful for patients who have complex presentations that involve social stressors, anxiety, and mood symptoms in conjunction with their physical symptoms. Interestingly, most patients describe both psychiatric and physical complaints in their timelines—consistent with the known relationship among these symptoms.[3] In the sample dialogue, the clinician asks for the patient's permission in writing the timeline. Obtaining this permission is important to maximize the patient's participation and interest. Clinicians may also benefit from practicing a few times with more organized patients.

References

1. de la Vega I, Eikmeier V, Ulrich R, Kaup B. The mental timeline in a crossed-hands paradigm. *Exp Psychol.* 2016;63(6):326–332.
2. Simpson SA, Feinstein RE. Crisis intervention in integrated care. In: Feinstein RE, Connelly JV, Feinstein MS, eds. *Integrating Behavioral Health and Primary Care.* New York, NY: Oxford University Press; 2017:497–513.
3. Murphy KM, McGuire AP, Erickson TM, Mezulis AH. Somatic symptoms mediate the relationship between health anxiety and health-related quality of life over eight weeks. *Stress Health.* 2017;33(3):244–252.

24

Ask "How Come?" Instead of "Why?"
Vary Your Phrasing Slightly to Improve the Tone of the Interview

Setting

A clinical interview necessarily involves asking a series of questions to refine a diagnosis and tailor treatment. Over time, these questions grow fatiguing for the patient. Then when sensitive topic areas are explored—drug use or sexual activity, for example—there is a risk that the tired patient perceives the clinician's continued questions as judgmental or even accusatory. Maintaining rapport and continuing to solicit necessary information with a distressed, tired patient requires delicacy and skill on the part of the interviewer.

Technique

When ascertaining patient's motivations or explanations, avoid asking, "Why?" Instead, try asking, "How come?"

Sample Dialogue

Clinician: Your blood sugar is higher than usual today. How are your sugars at home?

Patient: You know, I've just stopped checking. I know I should check, but I've been bad about that lately.

Oh, how come?

Lots of things, I suppose. I've just been checking for so long that once in a while I get sick of it, and I want to stop. It's not like I make changes all the time based on those results anyways, so I feel there isn't a need to check so frequently.

Why This Works

Asking patients "Why?" is a valuable interviewing tool. This simple and open-ended question provides insight into the patient's reasoning, motivations, and health beliefs. The patient has the opportunity to elaborate on the history of illness without the strictures of repeated questions. Their response to this question is also helpful for assessing for an intact thought process when delirium or psychosis is suspected, as some patients may provide tangential, disorganized, or nonsensical responses when freed from the organizing influence of frequently posed questions.

However, asking "Why?" may be perceived as adversarial. Patients who are struggling with adherence or dangerous behaviors often understand the implications of their choices and feel bad about those choices. The clinician must be careful not to pester the patient into feeling even worse. Many people under stress are naturally prone to feeling blamed or accused, too. Clinicians themselves know the feeling well from their professional lives: the fear of blame affects health professionals facing safety inquiries and students training in high stress clinical environments.[1,2]

The clinician strives to develop a collaborative alliance with the patient in which both parties seek to understand how the patient arrived for treatment. Clinicians should strive to avoid aggressive statements that threaten the sense of compassion and positive emotion in the treatment relationship.[3] Asking "How come?" solicits similar information as "Why?" but is perceived as a less aggressive question. Perhaps this better perception arises from the phrase's longer length or more frequent soft vowel sounds. Perhaps the phrase is used less frequently and therefore less likely to be unconsciously associated with negative past experience by the patient. Regardless, patients are less likely to feel nagged or accused.

Final Thoughts

This technique demonstrates how seemingly small word choices substantially alter how we interact with one another. This technique is surprisingly resistant to overuse, but its utility depends on the clinician's motivation for asking the question. If the clinician is truly non-judgmental and asking the question for the patient's sake, most patients respond positively and honestly. But simply asking "How come?" instead of "Why?" is no substitution for a clinician's authenticity and genuine altruism.

References

1. Health Quality Ontario. Patient safety learning systems: a systematic review and qualitative synthesis. *Ont Health Technol Assess Ser*. 2017;17(3):1–23.
2. Yildiz Findik U, Ozbas A, Cavdar I, Yildizeli Topcu S, Onler E. Assessment of nursing students' stress levels and coping strategies in operating room practice. *Nurse Educ Pract*. 2015;15(3):192–195.
3. Kubany ES, Richard DC, Bauer GB, Muraoka MY. Verbalized anger and accusatory "you" messages as cues for anger and antagonism among adolescents. *Adolescence*. 1992;27(107):505–516.

25

Observe Caregivers' Nonverbal Cues

Gather Information From Caregivers to Increase Accuracy and Efficiency in the Diagnosis of Cognitive Disorders

JOLEEN SUSSMAN, PHD, ABPP

Setting

Cognitive disorders like dementia may be missed in brief clinical encounters, as many patients with these disorders do not report an accurate history. For example, a patient may say that they are great drivers while a caregiver may report the patient has had driving accidents or close calls.[1] Brief cognitive tests are insufficient for diagnosis of dementia as they do not assess functional abilities. Incorporating collateral information from caregivers or loved ones is thus critically important to address these diagnostic challenges. While it is helpful for informants to accompany the patient, the clinician must be sensitive in soliciting collateral information when caregivers and loved ones feel uncomfortable contradicting the patient in their presence.

The Technique

When asking questions about functional abilities in the setting of possible cognitive impairment, pay attention to the nonverbal responses of the patient's loved ones who are present. Patients may report that they are driving safely, cooking on their own, or maintaining the home. Yet as they say these things, caregivers may shake their head, roll their eyes, or hold back a laugh as if in disbelief. These data are meaningful and imply another story. Before asking the caregiver their perspective, ask the patient permission to collect collateral data: "Can I ask your loved one some questions?" Patients most often agree. If they do not, ask the patient their concerns and let the caregiver know that you are always reachable outside the visit should concerns arise.

Sample Dialogue

Clinician: It seems you have missed several appointments in the past month. Is everything okay?

Patient: Yep, OK!

> Missing appointments is unlike you. I'm concerned about your forgetfulness. Since your wife is here, can we talk about how things are going day to day? Any car accidents or close calls lately?

> Nope, I've been driving trucks since I was 16, I'm a great driver.

> That is a long time. I see your wife smiling. Can I ask her how you're doing?

> Well, I guess, but you should be worried about her driving!

> Has your husband been in recent accidents or close calls?

> Well...

> OK, say, do you let your grandchildren ride with your husband?

> Oh, no, not anymore.

Why This Works

Clinicians should collect functional data from collateral informants to improve detection of dementia. Relaying solely on patient self-reports and cognitive testing decreases the accuracy of a cognitive disorder diagnosis.[2] A person with dementia rarely intentionally misleads clinicians about their abilities. Rather, the disease limits insight into their impairments. Patients who are well spoken, well dressed, and have maintained social graces may better hide cognitive impairment during brief encounters. Impairments are often uncovered upon gathering more information from loved ones.

When working with collateral informants, the clinician must apply finesse in gathering sensitive history related to the patient's independence—for example, their ability to drive, live alone, or manage finances. The clinician needs this information while maintaining rapport with the patient and not introducing conflict between the patient and their loved ones. Diving into collateral information gathering too quickly or without permission may upset patients, rupture rapport, and miss important data. Caregivers will be reluctant to disclose information under these circumstances. Gently asking permission and attending to the caregiver's nonverbal cues allows faster information gathering without blatantly calling out discrepancies. Caregivers who show nonverbal responses implying the patient's report to be inaccurate are often open to providing more information either within the visit or later via telephone, email, or secure messaging systems.

This technique is not without shortcomings. Given the negative stigma and potential loss of independence associated with dementia, some patients feel embarrassed by questions of functioning no matter how tactfully and gently asked. Furthermore, due to the lack of insight in some forms of cognitive impairment, some patients show frustration toward loved ones who share sensitive information that leads to recommendations against driving or independent living. Family member's nonverbal cues are a discreet way for the clinician to incorporate collateral without being confrontational. When the patient appears stressed or emotional about questions of functioning, the clinician should consider ceasing this line of questioning.

Final Thoughts

Clinicians are often rightfully focused on gathering content during the interview. Yet important information can be gathered by attending to the nonverbal affect and demeanor of the patient and their friends, family, or caregivers who are present. A skillful interviewer collects information not just with their ears but also with their eyes and attention to the interaction's emotional tenor. Broadening the senses during the encounter allows for richer and more efficient data collection. The evidence underlying this technique is strongest for patients with cognitive disorders, but this approach is valuable for soliciting collateral information in the treatment of any patient who may be an unreliable reporter (e.g., adolescents or patients with substance use disorders).

References

1. Brown LB, Ott BR, Papandonatos GD, Sui Y, Ready RE, Morris JC. Prediction of on-road driving performance in patients with early Alzheimer's disease. *J Am Geriatr Soc.* 2005;53(1):94–98.
2. Cacchione PZ, Powlishta KK, Grant EA, Buckles VD, Morris JC. Accuracy of collateral source reports in very mild to mild dementia of the Alzheimer type. *J Am Geriatr Soc.* 2003;51(6):819–823.

26

Roll With Impaired Reality Testing

Provide a Validating and Grounded Interview for Patients With Psychotic Symptoms

ERIN O'FLAHERTY, MD

Setting

A patient's impaired reality testing can make a clinical interview extremely challenging. Symptoms of impaired reality testing include delusional thinking, hallucinations, and disorganized thought content. These symptoms are often exhibited by patients who are suffering from an acute exacerbation of a psychotic illness like schizophrenia. Even the most experienced clinician may find themselves at a loss for words when speaking with a patient suffering from psychosis. Developing rapport with and collecting a history from patients experiencing psychosis requires a deft approach.

The Technique

As with any patient, an interview with a person experiencing psychosis begins with general questions about their symptoms. Psychotic symptoms may be evident from the beginning of the interview or may become apparent only after a few minutes of interaction. The clinician should maintain a calm and open demeanor regardless of the nature of the information being shared by the patient. This equanimity can be difficult given the sometimes bizarre information provided by a patient. However, a non-judgmental atmosphere will invite the patient to share further information.

More focused questions specific to the patient's experience should follow regardless of whether the history provided by the patient is grounded in reality or not. Follow-up questions help the clinician gather necessary information, observe the patient's thought process, and foster a working alliance. Questions such as, "What are the voices saying?" or "Who exactly is following you?" are appropriate. Avoid challenging the patient's version of reality by making contradictory statements—"I don't think anyone is following you," or "I don't think that's possible." Challenging their reality is not likely to be productive and undermines the therapeutic relationship. Your goal is to meet the patient where they are and understand their experience.

Instead of challenging psychotic symptoms, roll with the patient's reality. Validate the patient's experience of their symptoms and ask for details. Statements such as, "I understand why you are afraid," or "I can see why that would bother you" are appropriate. However, do not support that the psychotic content is real or make accommodations for psychotic thoughts. For example, it is not helpful to say, "I won't call you at home since your phones are being tapped."

Sample Dialogue

> Patient: My apartment isn't safe, I can't go back there.

> Clinician: How come?

> The government implanted microchips in my arm; they want me to go on a secret mission.

> OK—how long have you had these thoughts?

> I don't know, but the voices are talking so loudly. Can you hear them? They want you to join, too.

> I don't hear them, but I do understand why hearing those voices is bothering you. What are the voices saying?

> They're coming to get me; they're listening on the phone.

> How do these voices make you feel?

> Not safe, I'm not safe.

> I can see why what is happening is so scary for you.

Why This Works

Impaired reality testing makes data-gathering and rapport-building difficult. The experience of a patient with acute psychosis often involves delusions and hallucinations beyond the patient's control. Sometimes psychotic content is not clearly distinguished from reality; some psychotic content even involves the clinician. Moreover, patients with acute psychosis can become anxious, scared, angry, or desperate as a result of their thought content. Nevertheless, the clinician's goal with the patient experiencing psychosis is no different than with any other patient: set the patient at ease, develop trust, and make an assessment to guide treatment.

These objectives are best achieved not by confronting, but rather adjusting for, the patient's distorted sense of reality. The clinician does not need to shy away from a discussion of the psychotic symptoms themselves; asking pointed questions will not provoke the symptoms and is necessary to understand the patient's perspective. But the clinician's ability to roll with these symptoms without emotional excitement is also imperative to a successful clinical interaction. Maintaining a calm environment not only improves the quality of the interaction but is important for the general wellbeing of the patient. Patients with schizophrenia fare worse in social settings with high levels of emotional expression and excitability.[1]

The clinician's aim is to understand the patient's world without providing credence to symptoms or, worse, becoming incorporated in the patient's psychosis. A patient may ask for a reality-check that a delusion or hallucination is not real, or reassurance that they are safe. In that circumstance, it is appropriate to provide genuine feedback and reassurance. It is also appropriate to be truthful if a patient asks whether you are experiencing hallucinations or paranoia (as did the clinician in the sample dialogue).

Psychotic symptoms are not volitional and are not amenable to reassurances to the contrary—no matter how insistent the clinician. A more effective approach is remaining non-judgmental, validating the patient's experience, and avoiding collusion with psychotic symptoms. What matters in this situation is not whether what the patient is saying has basis in reality, but how their current beliefs and experiences impact emotions and behaviors.

Generally, psychotherapy helps patients with psychosis achieve better symptom control, social interactions, and life functioning.[2] Cognitive behavior therapy (CBT) in particular helps patients with schizophrenia apply coping strategies to ameliorate their symptoms.[3] The clinician's calm demeanor models for the patient affective stability despite the presence of stressful thoughts.[4] The patient in the sample dialogue has already benefitted from being able to mirror the clinician's even-keeled approach to their psychotic symptoms and might further benefit from behavioral coping skills to manage their intense feelings of fear. Eventually, using more advanced CBT techniques, the patient might learn how to "reality check" their perception of delusional content such as the government having implanted a microchip in their arm. This level of insight requires extended treatment (perhaps over years) with a trusted clinician.

Final Thoughts

The clinician walks a fine line when working with psychotic symptoms: concerned and curious, but not confrontational. This technique is unlikely to help with patients who are too disorganized in their speech and thought process to coherently converse. A better approach for more disorganized patients is to give them a few minutes to speak in order to assess their patterns of speech, psychotic themes, and affect. In this instance, there is less to be gained from the patient's symptom reporting or a traditional symptom checklist. The clinician should also keep in mind that not all psychotic symptoms are due to schizophrenia. In fact, many patients experience psychosis caused by personality, anxiety, or substance use disorders.[5,6]

References

1. Butzlaff RL, Hooley JM. Expressed emotion and psychiatric relapse: a meta-analysis. *Arch Gen Psychiatry.* 1998;55(6):547–552.
2. Bjornestad J, Veseth M, Davidson L, et al. Psychotherapy in psychosis: experiences of fully recovered service users. *Front Psychol.* 2018;9:1675.

3. Khoury B, Lecomte T, Gaudiano BA, Paquin K. Mindfulness interventions for psychosis: a meta-analysis. *Schizophr Res.* 2013;150(1):176–184.

4. Turkington D, Dudley R, Warman D, Beck A. Cognitive-behavioral therapy for schizophrenia: a review. *Focus.* 2006;2(2):223–233.

5. Pierre JM. Hallucinations in nonpsychotic disorders: toward a differential diagnosis of "hearing voices". *Har Rev Psychiatry.* 2010;18(1):22–35.

6. Srisurapanont M, Arunpongpaisal S, Wada K, Marsden J, Ali R, Kongsakon R. Comparisons of methamphetamine psychotic and schizophrenic symptoms: a differential item functioning analysis. *Neuropsychopharmacol Biol Psychiatry.* 2011:35(4);959–964.

27

Ask for Help Understanding

Frame an Open-Ended Question as a Plea for the Patient's Assistance

Setting

Sometimes patients present confusing histories and conflicting goals. It is human nature to misunderstand one another. When this happens in the clinician-patient relationship, the adverse burden of misunderstanding falls disproportionately on the clinician. After all, clinicians are expected to assemble the history, form a diagnosis, and dispense a treatment recommendation. This pressure to understand the patient belies the collaborative and patient-centered nature of the healing relationship. The clinician must tactfully engage the patient's help in resolving any confusion over the history or uncertainty in treatment goals.

The Technique

Use the phrase, "Help me understand . . ." to reposition the patient as the definitive source for history and goal setting. This phrase can be re-introduced throughout the interview whenever the clinician feels confused about what the patient is trying to say, their motivations for treatment, their goals for the therapeutic relationship, or anything else.

Sample Dialogue

Patient: I like the idea of not having to change my diet, even though I know it's good for me, but then if you're saying a medication might help, well, maybe that's the way to go. Who knows how badly I need to do anything. My parents were always on medication so that makes a difference to me. Then meds are all different nowadays…

Clinician: Sorry, we were talking about whether to start a medication for your blood pressure but I'm not sure I understand your thoughts here. Help me understand how you are making this decision around starting a medication.

> Sorry I sometimes ramble when I'm worrying! I'm definitely concerned about my blood pressure and want to make the right decision. First, I'm worried about medications.

> How so?

Why This Works

Perfectly clear communication between the clinician and patient will not always happen. Patients are worried about their health and unfamiliar with the treatment options; clinicians are trying to carefully provide care in a busy clinic for many patients. Communication breakdowns are inevitable.

This technique positions the patient as teacher (as indeed they are). And it relieves the clinician of the unobtainable expectation of omnisciently organizing the patient's history or discerning their treatment goals. The sample dialogue opens with a patient equivocating over a medication decision by alluding to numerous factors—the appeal of alternative treatments, questions over the urgency of change, concerns regarding medications. Rather than try to unpack these statements, the clinician re-organizes the discussion by reminding the patient of the question and soliciting the patient's help: "Help me understand what you are thinking." Whereas the patient may have been thinking aloud before, they are now instructed to communicate clearly and thereby teach the clinician. The patient is afforded the freedom of an open-ended question and, in responding, provides the clinician helpful clues as to their thinking.[1] For example, that the sample patient describes their emotional state is evidence as to the seriousness felt over this decision and a strong rapport with the clinician.

In the quest to realize patient-centered communication,[2] many clinicians feel that their role is one of a concierge in which they offer options for the patient to select. Certainly, this arrangement is part of the treatment relationship. A more holistic description of collaborative treatment relationships might further include the sense of shared responsibility between the patient and clinician. Patient-centered relationships place a great deal of responsibility on the patient to identify goals, weigh choices, and communicate effectively. Such collaborative communication contributes to more effective and safer treatment. Clinicians sometimes must be more pro-active on behalf of patients who lack the ability or capacity to assert this responsibility.

Final Thoughts

Even if clinicians sometimes feel that they are doing all the work in treatment, in fact, patients do more. Besides having the onus of being sick, patients are expected to play an active role in treatment planning albeit without the clinician's expertise. But just as there is an imbalance of medical knowledge between the clinician and patient, there is an imbalance of personal knowledge about the patient: the patient best understands their own history and preferences. Guiding patients through decision-making sometimes requires reminding them that they need to help the clinician understand their thought process. Communication is a two-way street, and neither the clinician nor patient are driving alone.

References

1. Teutsch C. Patient-doctor communication. *Med Clin North Am.* 2003;87(5):1115–1145.
2. Institute of Medicine (US) Committee on Quality of Health Care in America. *Crossing the Quality Chasm: A New Health System for the 21st Century.* Washington, DC: National Academy of Sciences; 2001.

28

Collect the Social History First
Re-Order the Traditional Interview to Better Engage Reluctant Patients

SARAH SCHRAUBEN, MD

Setting

The clinical interview does not always come naturally; some patients are more difficult to engage than others. Engagement can be particularly challenging if the patient has been brought to care by somebody else—an adolescent brought in by a parent, or an emergency room patient brought in by ambulance. Clinicians need a strategy to engage the reluctant patient.

The Technique

Rather than beginning the interview with the chief complaint, start with the social history. Let your patient know that before asking about symptoms and medications, you want to know them as a person first. This approach helps the patient feel comfortable in the interview and also provides important data. Some suggestions for opening questions are provided in Table 28.1. Maintaining a well-documented social history in the medical record allows the clinician to revisit the history at subsequent appointments and update key elements over time. This technique can be especially helpful for children and adolescents who are often slow to open up.

Sample Dialogue

Clinician: Before we talk about what brought you and your mom here today, I'd like to get to know you a bit. What do you do for fun?

Patient: I don't know. Hang out with friends, I guess.

> When you hang out with friends, what do you do?

Go to the mall, have sleepovers. But I haven't done that in a while.

> Why not?

I don't feel like it. And my mom's car's broken, so she can't drive me.

> Hmmm…That must be rough. Are there particular people in your life you feel like you can turn to when you're having a tough time?

No. My boyfriend broke up with me last month, and now I don't have anyone to talk to.

Why This Works

For many people, talking with a clinician can be intimidating. Discussing the details of one's inner life and private experiences can feel very uncomfortable especially if someone has not done it before. This technique encourages the clinician to build a treatment relationship by talking about familiar topics in a manner similar to how people first introduce themselves to one another in non-clinical settings. But unlike a casual introduction, more pointed questions will follow to put the patient's symptoms into context. Did the patient's anxiety and panic start at the same time as major changes in the home? Does the patient have people in their life that are supportive, or do they feel isolated?

Establishing solid rapport as soon as possible in the encounter pays dividends in gathering higher quality information with greater efficiency. A patient who feels supported by the clinician is more likely to speak frankly about symptoms that are difficult to discuss. The patient will also be more cooperative later in the interview should the clinician need to be more directive in gathering the history. An interview that begins with a social history helps the clinician contextualize the patient's symptoms into their rich, unique life and experiences. Some patients have been interviewed many times and develop a tendency to perfunctorily recite symptoms; beginning with the social history revitalizes these patients' interest in the encounter. The patient benefits from knowing that the clinician cares about them as an individual rather than as a set of symptoms. Knowing more about the patient's interests and home life also helps the clinician feel engaged and connected to the patient. When a patient is disengaged, the clinician is prone to disengage from the interview as well—and further alienate the patient.

Clinicians have good reason to be attentive to the patient's social environment. In the example above, the clinician learned details about the patient's social and family world that are important for understanding medical and psychiatric risks. The presence of anhedonia was quickly revealed, and a disruption in a romantic relationship may pose risks of depression, anxiety, or suicidal thoughts.[1,2] The information gathered through the social history provides information about the accessibility of various

Table 28.1 Questions to include in the social history

- "Who do you live with? Any changes in your household lately?" Follow-up questions might include the quality of relationship with others in the home as well as conflict among other household members.
- "What does your mom/dad/caregiver/partner do for work? What's their schedule like?" Understanding the availability of the patient's support persons will impact any potential treatment plan.
- "What stressful things are going on in your family right now? How does your family cope with stress?" This question ascertains the resiliency of the patient's social network.
- "Do you feel like you have enough support in your life now, or do you wish you had more?" Social support, or even perceived social support, has an effect on the patient's quality of life and ability to overcome adverse life events.
- For follow-up appointments, begin the visit by asking about topics that arose during the previous visit's social history. "How's your new job going?" "Last time we met, your grandmother was sick. How is she doing?"

---

treatment options. If this patient does not have access to reliable transportation, how will they get medications refilled? Is it realistic to attend regular appointments? Some family environments—for example, those with high expressed emotion—are especially challenging and increase the likelihood of psychiatric complications.[3]

Final Thoughts

For any clinician who is treating a patient, the clinical interview is critical in establishing a treatment relationship. At times, collecting the social history first may make the clinician feel rushed compared to starting interviews with the chief complaint. (Is this information *really* important?) In discussing interests and hobbies, some patients may become excited and digressive. This, in and of itself, is useful clinical information. The patient's tangential thought process may suggest certain diagnoses. It can also provide clues as to how this patient is likely to manage interpersonal relationships generally. In the end, the clinician's attention will be rewarded: a solid alliance between a clinician and patient improves patient outcomes for various conditions, from low back pain to depression.[4,5]

It is not unusual for children to return with pictures or mementos mentioned during a previous visit, or for an adult to express appreciation for being listened to. Unfortunately, for many patients and especially children who present in psychiatric settings, it is unusual to have had the experience of being listened to carefully by someone who is genuinely interested. This technique helps make the clinical interview feel therapeutic.

References

1. Sands A, Thompson EJ, Gaysina D. Long-term influences of parental divorce on offspring affective disorders: a systematic review and meta-analysis. *J Affect Disord.* 2017;218:105–114.
2. Kazan D, Calear AL, Batterham PJ. The impact of intimate partner relationships on suicidal thoughts and behaviours: a systematic review. *J Affect Disord.* 2016;190:585–598.
3. Hooley JM. Expressed emotion and relapse of psychopathology. *Annu Rev Clin Psychol.* 2007;3:329–352.

4. Ferreira PH, Ferreira ML, Maher CG, Refshauge KM, Latimer J, Adams RD. The therapeutic alliance between clinicians and patients predicts outcome in chronic low back pain. *Phys Therapy*. 2013:93(4):470–478.
5. Krupnick JL, Stosky SM, Simmens S, et al. The role of the therapeutic alliance in psychotherapy and pharmacotherapy outcome: findings in the national institute of mental health treatment of depression collaborative research program. *J Consult Clin Psychol*. 1996:64(3):532–539.

29

Ask About Family History
Use the Family History as a Lead-in to Sensitive Questions

Setting

Many patients are reluctant to share sensitive information with clinicians they do not know, particularly about substance use and mental health issues. Since the family history must be collected regardless, why not use it as a lead-in to ask about these sensitive topics.

The Technique

Many clinicians separate the family history from the rest of the interview, almost as an afterthought for which they need to check a box. Instead, leverage questions about family history to normalize sensitive conditions and facilitate obtaining a comprehensive history.

Sample Dialogue

> Clinician: Is there a history of suicides or suicide attempts in your family?

> Patient: Actually, my grandfather was in an institution and eventually killed himself.

> Your grandfather completed suicide. I'm sorry to hear that. Have *you* ever hurt yourself intentionally?

Why This Works

The family history works well as a lead-in to sensitive topics, because it normalizes the presence of those topics in the context of a question the patient is expecting to hear anyway. Patients who might be reluctant to disclose their own history will freely talk about others'; once that door is open, step through it by extending your interview to the patient's own history. The sample dialogue uses a question about suicide, but this technique could introduce questions about substance use and legal history, for example. This technique is also helpful because the clinician gains insight into the patient's upbringing and risk factors for potential diagnoses as well.

A good family history adds value to the clinical interview. For example, a patient with a family history of mania, schizophrenia, or lithium treatment is at higher risk for bipolar depression—a condition that requires different treatment than unipolar depression.[1] Patients with a family history of suicide are at increased risk for impulsivity, interpersonal dysfunction, self-harm, and suicide themselves.[2] Asking about the family history helps the clinician better understand the patient's background and upbringing. The family history might also inform the patient's thoughts, fears, and preferences around treatment. Clinicians can gain a more complete and personal sense of their patients, while patients feel better understood.

In the above dialogue, the family history raises many more questions that might be explored. What psychiatric illness did this patient's grandfather have that resulted in long term hospitalization? Did other family members have serious mental illness? The interviewer validates the patient's response in a general way. The alternatives of responding, "I'm sorry to hear that," or "I imagine that was difficult for your family," would have been more affective statements that would also work here. That the patient's response carried so much information is a reminder to avoid relegating the family history to the end of the interview, as it may reveal significant information requiring time to explore in detail.

Final Thoughts

This technique can save time in the interview: if you have to ask a family history anyway, you might as well use it to also build rapport and give you clues to the diagnoses all at once. But not all patients can speak benignly about their families of origin. Some patients do not want to be associated with conditions or events among their family, in which case this technique is hardly benign. The clinician can validate that the patient is upset and pursue a different approach to acquiring information. Such reactions can be invaluable for understanding the patient's background, preferences, and fears around treatment.

References

1. Manning JS. Tools to improve differential diagnosis of bipolar disorder in primary care. *Prim Care Companion J Clin Psychiatry*. 2010;12(Suppl 1):17–22.
2. Rajalin M, Hirvikoski T, Renberg ES, Asberg M, Jokinen J. Family history of suicide and interpersonal functioning in suicide attempters. *Psychiatry Res*. 2017;247:310–314.

30

Wonder Aloud With the Patient

Use and Re-Use a Brief, Non-Committal Phrase to Explore the Patient's History and Treatment Options

Setting

Clinicians must exhibit curiosity about our patients' lives. With patients, curiosity helps in soliciting a history and forming a diagnosis. From a professional standpoint, clinical curiosity drives continued clinical growth. Sometimes it feels as though all the curiosity in a conversation lies with the clinician. Clinicians have all experienced this point in a patient encounter: the patient feels tired or irritable with endless questions, and the clinician gets the sense that this relationship is an entirely one-sided affair in which the clinician is working harder than the patient. The ennui is stultifying for patients and exhausting for clinicians. The clinician must be prepared to re-introduce the sense of collaboration and mutual interest into the encounter.

The Technique

Make a statement in which you ask, "I wonder . . ." This phrase might introduce a specific question or test a possible hypothesis. Or the clinician might test the acceptability of a treatment recommendation. The patient often takes advantage of this open-ended question to provide greater detail or entertain the proposed idea; they are not committed to the idea any more than the clinician. It is not unsound to try this technique again in response: for example, validate the patient's response, and wonder aloud again.

Sample Dialogue

Patient: Every time I get near the hospital, I feel anxious. My hands get clammy. I feel on edge. I'm not sure. I don't think of myself as a nervous person. But I've started even changing how I drive to work to avoid this neighborhood.

Clinician: It sounds like your anxiety is even changing how you commute. I wonder what it is you start thinking when you're anxious.

> Well, once I start, there are lots of things I worry about, but it always starts with me remembering that car accident where I had to go to the ER in an ambulance. I was so scared!

> An accident like that would be scary for anyone, but then I wonder if you have considered whether you might benefit from talking with someone about that traumatic experience.

Why This Works

This technique is helpful in several ways. Most simply, it helps the clinician vary their phrasing during longer clinical interviews. To repeatedly answer questions can be a tiring experience for patients (and often monotonous for clinicians). Of course, questions are a necessary part of clinical medicine, but they are limited. Most questions that clinicians ask—How long did this last? Where does it hurt?—do not invite much thoughtfulness from patients. Ironically, clinicians then grow frustrated when patients' answers are insufficiently thorough, too vague, or confusing. Many questions come across as leading, and patients who are eager to please may have difficulty being truthful on sensitive subjects. (For example, "You don't drink much alcohol, do you?") When the patient does answer all these questions, responsibility for interpreting the answers rests entirely on the clinician.

The phrase "I wonder" invites the patient to be a partner in this discussion while also varying the pace and style of the clinical interview. This technique is common among psychodynamic clinicians who hope to explore patient's unconscious motivations. "I wonder" does not presume any particular judgment or opinion by the clinician. The phrase does not even presume a response from the patient; rather, the patient shares the onus of exploring the history and considering solutions. The interview begins to feel more like the patient's voice than the clinician's. In psychodynamic psychotherapy, the clinician maintains a stance that ranges from supportive to expressive.[1] A supportive position include giving frank advice to the patient; this position reveals the clinician's opinion and subjects the clinician to the patient's approval, disappointment, and other transference reactions. In contrast, more expressive interventions utilize previously unconscious material to help the patient understand behaviors, thoughts, and feelings. Uncovering this material relies on the clinician's neutral stance and the patient's free associations. This technique allows clinicians to ask questions without losing that neutral, expressive position.

No matter how neutral the clinician hopes to be, patients will inevitably project ideas and opinions on their clinician. The clinician in the sample dialogue begins by validating the patient's report and using an "I wonder" phrase. The patient discloses a history of re-experiencing relating to a traumatic episode that should make the clinician immediately suspicious for post-traumatic stress disorder. The clinician again validates the patient's perspective by normalizing this response before continuing to re-apply the technique and introduce the possibility of psychotherapy. The clinician has not conveyed any opinion as to the importance or indication for treatment. But the patient answers, "maybe you're right." The patient's response suggests that treatment is being recommended (the clinician said no such thing) and that they are open to treatment. At the end of this dialogue, it will be the patient who has done the heavy lifting and offered a commitment to pursue treatment. There is no hard sell by the clinician.

Final Thoughts

A lot of responsibility is placed on clinicians: be kind, be smart, be up-to-date, get the right diagnosis, deliver the right treatment. These expectations are set by our profession and society but are difficult to apply one patient at a time in the treatment room.[2] Even so, in the clinical interview the clinician is never more than half of the team. The clinician has thus one more responsibility that makes all the others easier—to help the patient take part in the healing alliance. Cultivating the patient's participation is easier with a skillful interview that gives the patient an opportunity to wonder aloud.

References

1. Gabbard GO. *Psychodynamic Psychiatry in Clinical Practice.* 5th edition. Washington, DC: American Psychiatric Publishing; 2014.
2. Ivers N, Barnsley J, Upshur R, et al. "My approach to this job is . . . one person at a time": perceived discordance between population-level quality targets and patient-centred care. *Can Fam Physician.* 2014;60(3):258–266.

III
Making an Assessment

31
Track Symptoms and Behaviors
Keep a Log to Aid Diagnosis and Begin Treatment

The Setting

The clinical interview occurs at a single moment in time yet attempts to capture a history of events that occur in the past, in different places, under wholly different conditions than in the clinician's office. We depend on patients' and caregivers' memories to give an account of events, but memory can be influenced—and impaired—by emotional valence, biases, and illness.[1] Then when the clinician asks more and increasingly specific questions of the patient's history, it feels that ever more contradictions and uncertainties arise.

The Technique

Teach the patient to track their symptoms and bring a reporting log to their next appointment. The patient can track symptoms, certain behaviors, moods, or any other focus of the visit. A sample tracking log is shown in Table 31.1. The simplest way to track symptoms is to list the number of times something happens every day. In Table 31.1, column A lets the patient mark which days they went for a walk. A slightly more sophisticated symptom log might also include column B (a description of why they did not go for a walk) or column C (a description of what helped them be successful). For another patient, perhaps a log would include the occurrence of a particular symptom (e.g., nausea), how long it lasted, and what was going on when the symptom started. This technique is valuable for myriad health behaviors and symptoms—medication adherence, diet, or sleep. One might even "prescribe" this homework as described in chapter 48. When the patient returns for their follow-up visit, the clinician should prioritize review of the tracking log.

Sample Dialogue

Patient: I really want to start walking again, I know how much it would help my numbers and my weight.

Clinician: What would walking again look like for you?

Well, I just want to walk around the neighborhood after dinner, maybe for 20 minutes or so. Nothing too crazy.

That sounds like a great goal. What in particular gets in the way of you doing that ?

Not much. It's getting cold again so that will make it harder, but I don't mind the cold. And I have really good boots.

You've put a lot of effort into thinking about this. I wonder if it would be worth tracking your progress as a way to get more information as to what gets in the way of meeting your goal to walk more.

What do you mean by tracking?

It means noting down the times you walk or don't walk and what's going on for you in each situation. We'll create a tracking sheet for you to use. Sometimes just tracking makes it easier to change behaviors, so I think this could be really helpful for you.

Why This Works

Tracking behaviors and feelings is a staple of many psychotherapies and particularly cognitive behavior therapy. Symptom tracking is used in several ways. Tracking allows a more accurate reporting of the patient's experiences. Many patients actually over-report symptoms during clinical visits and still others under-report.[1] Patients who are prone to over-reporting may be surprised to see how infrequently symptoms occur. Moreover, the inclusion of nuanced details in more complex tracking logs—details like the duration and precipitants of symptoms, or barriers to certain behaviors—allows the patient to remember significantly more about that specific episode.[2] These additional details aid in diagnosis and treatment.

The act of tracking not only enables patients to recall more detail but also changes the frequency of those behaviors and symptoms. A classic example of this phenomenon is seen in dieting. Dieters are often instructed to write down what they eat. Knowing that consumption will be recorded and reviewed keeps the desired behavior change foremost in the dieter's mind and in this way effects that very change. In social and medical research, the term Hawthorne Effect describes the propensity of research subjects to alter their behaviors when they are being observed.[3]

Moreover, this technique encourages the patient to participate more in their evaluation and treatment. Clinicians often feel pressured to take responsibility for obtaining an accurate history or helping the patient change behaviors when in fact memory is quite fallible and change, difficult. Using a symptom or behavior log as part of treatment re-introduces the importance of collaboration into the clinical encounter.

Table 31.1 A sample behavior tracking log

	A	B	C
	Did I go for a walk?	*What kept me from going?*	*What helped me go?*
Monday	Yes		My wife came with me.
Tuesday	No	Football game was on.	
Wednesday	Yes		Felt bad that I watched football instead yesterday.

Table 31.2 Example elements that can be included in a tracking log

	Examples	*Additional elements to track*
Physical symptoms	• Headaches • Nausea • Fatigue	• What were you doing or how were you feeling when this started? • How long did this last?
Psychiatric symptoms	• Mood • Hallucinations • Anxiety • Sleep	• How intense were the symptoms (e.g., 1–10)? • Where were the symptoms located? • What did the symptoms keep you from doing? • What helped you feel better?
Behaviors	• Medication adherence • Exercise • Diet	• How did you feel afterwards? • What helped you complete the behaviors? • How often did you do these things? For how long?

Final Thoughts

Tracking logs are very adaptable and can be modified to suit any symptom or behavior. Table 31.2 describes examples of information that might be collected in a log; the content depends on the situation, what would be valuable for the clinician, and what is important to the patient. Symptom tracking can be done on paper or via online tools and phone apps. Two important elements of introducing tracking should not be forgotten. First, the clinician needs to be committed to the importance of this technique. If the patient senses that this is merely an obligation without benefit, they will not participate. Secondly, it is vital for the clinician to start the next visit by reviewing the log. To neglect the patient's work is to invalidate their efforts and, worse, lose its utility.

References

1. Van den Bergh O, Walentynowicz M. Accuracy and bias in retrospective symptom reporting. *Curr Opin Psychiatry*. 2016;29(5):302–308.
2. Brown GD, Neath I, Chater N. A temporal ratio model of memory. *Psychol Rev*. 2007;114(3):539–576.
3. Sedgwick P, Greenwood N. Understanding the Hawthorne effect. *BMJ*. 2015;351:h4672.

32

Find the Key Worry

Consider the Anxious Patient's Most Important Worry in Making the Diagnosis

Setting

Anxiety disorders are the most common psychiatric illnesses and affect around one-third of Americans over a lifetime.[1] Anxiety and anxiety disorders manifest with many different symptoms; changes in sleep, concentration, irritability, somatic symptoms, and mood are all common. Such variety does not make diagnosis and treatment easy. Additionally, patients with anxiety often report that something is wrong but have difficulty describing what exactly is bothering them. Clinicians in all settings must be familiar with putting together at least an initial differential diagnosis in patients with anxiety symptoms.

The Technique

When patients describe anxiety, focus on the most prominent thought that comes to the patient's mind when they are feeling anxious. Different ways to ask about this include pressing the patient to imagine what they think of first, or what they think of most often when they are feeling anxious. The patient may need to go home and track the thoughts that come up when they are anxious (as described in chapter 31). Patients who describe a great many thoughts at once might benefit from writing all those thoughts down, then selecting a thought among them about which they feel most strongly.

Sample Dialogue

Patient: When I'm at work, I always feel so worried. I'm jittery. I get sweaty. Sometimes I just leave my desk and hide out in the bathroom, or go home early and hope nobody notices.

Clinician: That doesn't sound comfortable. How often do you feel like this?

> It's starting to be every day now. I just worry so much.

> And when you start feeling really anxious, what is the first thought that comes to mind? I'm curious what you're thinking about.

> I worry that other people are judging me. Like I'm not good enough, or that people will look down on me, or realize that I'm a failure. I usually know that this isn't true, but sometimes it's difficult.

Why This Works

Anxiety disorders are difficult to diagnose based on diagnostic criteria contained in the Diagnostic and Statistical Manual (DSM-5).[2] These diagnoses are very heterogeneous: post-traumatic stress disorder (PTSD) has over 600,000 symptom combinations in the DSM-5![3] These disorders have a great deal of overlap with mood and somatic symptom disorders as well. Distinguishing among these great many possibilities and nuances within a brief clinical encounter is difficult but important. Anxiety disorders have very different treatments; for example, some somatic symptom disorders require regular medical visits, and benzodiazepines are contraindicated in the treatment of PTSD.[4]

Cognitive behavior therapists work to identify the most important cognitive distortion—sometimes called a "hot thought"—around which to build a therapeutic plan. This thought is typically the most distressing, most impairing dysfunctional thought pattern that is driving the patient's symptoms. Identifying the key worry is also helpful for discerning the particular anxiety-related diagnosis. Anxiety disorders vary crucially in their core cognitive distortions. While myriad different symptoms relate to anxiety, the hot thought is more likely distinct to the diagnosis. Table 32.1 lists some common hot thoughts found in common disorders characterized by anxiety and worry.

This single thought does not a diagnosis make. The clinician must consider the patient's reaction to this thought and the severity and duration of the resulting impairment. The sample dialogue demonstrates the clinician briefly validating the patient's concerns and then giving some simple instruction around how to identify a key worry. This patient describes a key fear of social situations and being judged, which is common among patients with social anxiety disorder. That is a natural place to start with this patient; a psychotherapist might use this particular hot thought as a starting point for an entire course of treatment. In a single brief clinical encounter, the clinician can at least gain a fair suspicion for the diagnosis. There is also therapeutic value to knowing this hot thought. Should the patient later feel agitated, this thought is likely the one driving symptoms. The clinician is able to help the patient de-escalate through offering more specific validation and normalization. (For example, "I know how scared you are of feeling judged, I would be anxious in your situation, too.")

Table 32.1 Common key worries in anxiety and anxiety-related disorders

Key worry	Disorder
I worry about trauma that I have experienced.	Post-traumatic stress disorder
I worry how others think or me, or of being embarrassed.	Social anxiety disorder
I worry about having another panic attack.	Panic disorder
I worry about a specific event or thing (e.g., snakes).	Specific phobia
I worry that my symptom is a deadly disease.	Illness anxiety disorder
I worry that I am worthless.	Depressive disorder (e.g., major depression, dysthymic disorder)
I worry about going into withdrawal.	Substance use disorder
I worry about people following me.	Psychotic disorder (e.g., delusional disorder, schizophrenia, or substance-induced psychosis)

Final Thoughts

Many non-psychiatric clinicians feel uncomfortable parsing the nuances of psychiatric diagnosis. In fact, even experienced psychiatrists are less focused on the specifics of DSM-5 diagnostic criteria then they are on the particular symptoms that are most impairing to the patient.[5] This technique helps identify impairing symptoms and enables treatment to begin, even if a formal diagnostic label has not yet been applied.

References

1. Bandelow B, Michaelis S. Epidemiology of anxiety disorders in the 21st century. *Dialogues Clin Neurosci.* 2015;17(3):327–335.
2. American Psychiatric Association. *Diagnostic and Statistical Manual of Mental Disorders: DSM-5.* 5th edition. Arlington, VA: American Psychiatric Association; 2013.
3. Galatzer-Levy IR, Bryant RA. 636,120 ways to have posttraumatic stress disorder. *Perspect Psychol Sci.* 2013;8(6):651–662.
4. Department of Veterans Affairs, Department of Defense. VA/DOD clinical practice guideline for the management of posttraumatic stress disorder and acute stress disorder: clinician summary. *VA/DoD Clinical Practice Guidelines 2017*; 2017. Accessed online December 20, 2018: www.healthquality.va.gov/guidelines/MH/ptsd/VADoDPTSDCPGClinicianSummaryFinal.pdf.
5. First MB, Rebello TJ, Keeley JW, et al. Do mental health professionals use diagnostic classifications the way we think they do? A global survey. *World Psychiatry.* 2018;17(2):187–195.

33

Consider Past Healthcare Encounters
Ask How Patients' Past Healthcare Experiences May Inform Their Current Experience

Setting

Most patients have had experiences within the healthcare system prior to their visit—these experiences have varied from poor to excellent. The patient's presentation and reactions to you and your visit are informed by past experiences.[1] It is useful to consider this when you find yourself confused about what is happening in the appointment, such as feeling uncomfortably idealized or unfairly villainized.[2]

The Technique

Ask the patient about their previous healthcare experiences. Explore what worked in these situations and what did not. Consider with the patient how their current healthcare experience is similar or different than those past encounters; validate challenges, and also highlight things that went well. Discuss how you and the patient can make your treatment relationship more effective based on those past experiences.

Sample Dialogue

> Clinician: We're talking about your lab results, and you seem upset. Can you tell me why?

> Patient: I don't know why I bother coming. No one ever helps me.

> I'm not sure what you mean, but I can tell you're upset. What has your experience been like in this clinic before today?

> People are always rushing me through. No one wants to listen to what's going on. They just want to check my blood pressure and labs and send me home.

Well, it's true that we need to check your blood pressure and labs. But I want you to be able to tell me about how you've been feeling, too. I'd like to plan our appointments in a way that best helps you.

Why This Works

Asking about the patient's past healthcare experiences affords insight into the patient's perspective of what has been helpful—or exasperating—for them. The clinician may learn how the patient reacts to different treatment settings and clinician styles. This information enables the clinician to create a more comfortable encounter. In the sample dialogue, the patient shares that they have felt rushed throughout prior appointments. These prior experiences have precipitated a sense of unease in the current one. The cue is clear: the clinician responds by inviting discussion around how appointments might be structured in a way that addresses the patient's agenda as well as other clinical items.

With clinician turnover being common,[3] patients sometimes develop an emotional connection to the healthcare institution rather than the clinician. This phenomenon has been described as institutional transference.[4] In psychodynamic therapy, transference describes the patient's emotional and personal reaction to the clinician. Institutional transference refers to the same reactions not towards individuals but towards institutions. A similar reaction is how persons feel loyalty to corporate brands, social organizations, and political groups. Institutional transference can unexpectedly complicate the clinician's efforts to build a therapeutic relationship.[5]

Understanding the patient's relationship to both the institution and the medical field as a whole helps the clinician anticipate complications in treatment. Particular attention should be paid to the patient's report of precipitous terminations in prior treatment relationships. These terminations are likely to recur without foresight by the clinician. Good questions to understand the patient's past treatment include, "How come you switched clinicians?" "How did treatment go with your prior clinician?" "How would you like for things to go differently here?" Based on the patient's responses, the clinician might be able to accommodate simple needs, such as the sample patient's request to discuss other content during appointments. At times more complex interventions might be indicated. For example, a clinician might realize they need to set early expectations around boundaries in order to work effectively with a more demanding patient; not doing so may lead to the patient's disappointment and the clinician's impaired empathy and effectiveness.

Final Thoughts

Unexpected reactions by patients during the encounter should raise suspicion that the patient is reacting to the clinician based on prior experiences in healthcare.[3] Soliciting a history of those experiences is helpful, but beware the patient who indiscriminately vents about all past negative healthcare experiences. This unfocused excessiveness is rarely useful and usually leads both patient and clinician to feel irritable. Once the clinician has a sense of the patient's experiences, politely but firmly interrupt the patient (perhaps using the technique in chapter 22) and refocus on that day's visit.

References

1. Sledge WH, Feinstein AR. A clinimetric approach to the components of the patient-physician relationship. *JAMA*. 1997;278(23):2043–2048.
2. Levy MS. A helpful way to conceptualize and understand reenactments. *J Psychother Pract Res*. 1998;7(3):227–235.
3. Beidas RS, Marcus S, Wolk CB, et al. A prospective examination of clinician and supervisor turnover within the context of implementation of evidence-based practices in a publicly-funded mental health system. *Adm Policy Men Health*. 2016;43(5):640–649.
4. Martin HP. Types of institutional transference. *Bull Menninger Clin*. 1989;53(1):58–62.
5. Gendel MH, Resier DE. Institutional countertransference. *Am J Psychiatry*. 1981;138(4):508–511.

34

Identify What Is Solvable

Focus on Concrete Objectives That You and the Patient Can Realistically Solve Together

Setting

Clinicians grow discouraged when patients present with seemingly endless complaints and requests. There are several reasons patients present with many concerns. For one, they simply have more. More Americans are living longer with multiple chronic conditions[1]; managing this co-morbidity demands busier appointments. Other reasons relate to the nature of the clinician-patient relationship. Some patients tend to understand clinicians' solicitations of an agenda as asking for new problems rather than existing problems, thereby lengthening the encounter's to-do list.[2] Other patients grow emotionally invested in the clinical relationship and fear abandonment, believing that the relationship may only exist with the persistence of multiple health concerns. Regardless of why the patient raises so many issues, the clinician can refocus the encounter by initiating a discussion about what is realistically solvable in the current visit.[3]

The Technique

Elicit the patient's chief complaint and make note of all concerns. Review with the patient their self-identified needs to validate their concerns and build the treatment alliance. Then focus with the patient on which complaints are addressable, or solvable, in the current appointment. "Which of these issues should we focus on solving today?" Reassure the patient that you understand they have many concerns and, at the same time, you will together make the most of the present encounter by addressing what is solvable.

Sample Dialogue

> Patient: I'm constipated, my blood pressure feels high, I hurt my shoulder, I haven't been checking my blood sugars, and my kids keep calling me for money.

> Clinician: I'm glad you were able to come in today; you have a lot of things on your mind. You mentioned you're constipated, concerned about your blood pressure and your sugars, you hurt your shoulder, and your kids keep calling you for money. Which of these concerns should we focus on solving today?

> Well, it's all bad. But I really want to focus on my shoulder, the rest of it hasn't changed much.

> That makes a lot of sense. Let's focus on what happened to your shoulder. We'll continue to work on the other things you brought up and revisit these concerns as we need to next time. How does this plan sound?

Why This Works

This technique introduces the importance of negotiating the goals of treatment in situations where the patient's expectations may not align with what the clinician can solve. The patient and clinician must share goals in order to be successful. This technique does not imply that the patient's many needs are insignificant. Quite the opposite: the clinician must start by validating all of the patient's concerns and building a treatment alliance. However, the clinician must also be forthright in what the encounter can produce. Issues may not be solvable because they are beyond the expertise of the clinician, require more time than available, or involve social and relationship issues unrelated to healthcare. In better focusing on issues that are solvable, the clinician sets realistic expectations while instilling hope in the patient that their problems can be helped. Furthermore, the clinician preserves their own sense of efficacy and avoids burnout.

This technique is most useful with patients with chronic conditions who are established in care and frequently bring in a long list of concerns. These patients sometimes give clinicians a sense that their relationship with the clinician is even more important than an improvement in symptoms; their ongoing symptoms must persist to perpetuate a caring relationship with the clinician. The clinician-patient relationship ceases to be treatment-oriented as the clinician becomes a sounding board for a litany of overwhelming social, interpersonal, and even existential concerns. The clinician develops a sense of defeat as the patient's problem list feels never-ending. Rather than grow resigned to or bored in a stale clinical encounter, focusing on what is solvable re-introduces a sense of action to the interview and reassures the patient that improved health will not jeopardize the relationship.

Agenda setting is an important element of cognitive behavior therapy (CBT). CBT clinicians, in collaboration with their patients, often make the session agenda explicit at the outset of every encounter, even detailing how many minutes will be spent on different items. Agenda setting engages the patient in prioritizing problems and taking ownership in how they would like to spend session time. In following an agenda, patients feel heard, important issues are not missed, and the encounter is as productive as possible.

Final Thoughts

Patients with multiple complaints may identify numerous disparate goals beyond the ability of the clinician to solve. Validating the patient's struggles and then focusing the encounter on what is solvable re-introduces a sense of efficacy and hope into the treatment relationship. Trouble arises when patients share only concerns that are not clearly solvable by the clinician—for example, housing, employment, or marital stress. In these situations, this technique applies much the same. Validate the patient's concerns and prioritize as necessary. The clinician should be prepared to acknowledge how these social stressors impact the patient's health even as a ready solution is not available. Nevertheless, the clinician agrees to continue meeting with the patient and offering support as able. In assuring the patient that they will continue to be seen, the clinician communicates to the patient that they will not be abandoned, regardless of the resolution (or not) of their complaints. With this technique, setting boundaries around what is solvable relieves the clinician of feeling the need to carry, and solve, all of the patient's burdens.

References

1. Buttorff C, Ruder T, Bauman M. *Multiple Chronic Conditions in the United States*. Santa Monica, CA: RAND Corporation; 2017. Accessed online December 8, 2018: www.rand.org/pubs/tools/TL221.html.
2. Robinson JD, Heritage J. How patients understand physicians' solicitations of additional concerns: implications for up-front agenda setting in primary care. *Health Commun.* 2016;31(4):434–444.
3. Strous RD, Ulman A, Kotler M. The hateful patient revisited: relevance for 21st century medicine. *Eur J Intern Med.* 2006;17(6):387–393.

35

Talk About Traits, Not Diagnosis
Think of Maladaptive Thoughts and Behaviors on a Spectrum of Normal

JODI ZIK, MD, AND MELANIE RYLANDER, MD

Setting

Patients are looking for our assistance, not our judgment. Every healthcare professional sees patients with maladaptive cognitions and habitual poor decision-making. Often these patterns are so entrenched as to be unconscious to the patient. In their most severe forms, a diagnosis of personality disorder may be present. Clinicians are taught to conceptualize illness through a categorical lens and apply a diagnosis for which there are recommended treatments. Yet psychiatric diagnoses are often inexact, and many patients have preconceived notions that make them averse to a psychiatric diagnosis. Some clinicians worry about alienating patients from treatment by disclosing a psychiatric diagnosis such as personality disorder or somatic symptom disorder.

The Technique

Apply an alternative framework to traditional psychiatric diagnosis by describing patients from a dimensional perspective.[1] A dimensional perspective focuses on understanding patient behaviors as variances of normal instead of ascribing diagnostic labels. Personality traits include extraversion, neuroticism, agreeableness, novelty seeking, harm avoidance, reward dependence, and perseverance. These traits are present to some degree in all persons.[2,3]

Explain to the patient how their patterns of behavior and decision-making processes fall along a continuum. This explanation—rather than reviewing diagnostic criteria and treatment options—is often more digestible and understandable for patients. The clinician can reframe a patient's maladaptive personality features as an extreme of normal rather than pathologic.

Sample Dialogue

> Patient: My wife is getting more frustrated with me over my inability to make decisions or take the initiative to do things on my own. I've always been like that though. Even as a kid, I relied on my mother to do everything. It's why I didn't want to move out until I got engaged. I've never felt like I could do anything on my own.

> Clinician: You're saying that feeling dependent on other people has been a long-standing personality feature.

> Basically, yeah, but my wife is really unhappy with me and says there's something wrong with me and that I need to change.

> What do you think?

> Well, I don't think I'm completely defective, but she's probably right about a lot of it.

> Everyone has the need to be cared for. That's normal, and we all depend on other people. It sounds like at times this normal need takes control of you and becomes a dominant feature of your personality. A lot of people have that tendency. If you think being more independent would help you, we can talk about ways to work on this.

Why This Works

The relative balance of personality traits constitutes personality.[2,3] Certain personality traits are enhanced or de-emphasized in adapting to the stressors of early attachment and environmental influences, but these changes may ultimately become maladaptive later in life.[1] Traditional diagnostic dogma suggests that extremes of normal are categorical diagnoses with specific constellations of symptoms and prescribed treatments. However, viewing patients categorically predisposes us to the inherent biases of these diagnoses, rendering us more susceptible to negative countertransference and stereotypes.[4] This susceptibility in turn inhibits our ability to see a patient as an individual with unique struggles and psychological dynamics. To counter this shortcoming of traditional psychiatric diagnoses and develop new treatment strategies, the National Institute of Mental Health developed the Research Domain Criteria (RDoC), a dimensional framework examining aspects of mental health and pathology along a spectrum as a complement to categorical diagnoses.[5] Table 35.1 describes some personality dimensions and their conceptualizations in RDoC.

In this sample dialogue, the patient describes a pattern of behavior that may be causing problems in life. However, instead of asking about further diagnostic criteria, the clinician asks about the patient's feelings of dependency. The clinician normalizes this feeling—"Everyone has the need to be cared for"—and points out how it underlies the

Table 35.1 Sample dimensions of personality

Dimension	Description	RDoC Conceptualization
Extroversion versus introversion	Preference for social activities versus isolation	Social communication
Reward seeking versus punishment avoidant	Motivation to attain new or positive outcomes versus evasion of change or negative outcomes	Behavioral motivation
Logic oriented versus emotion oriented	Orientation toward reasoning and critical thinking versus empathetic and compassionate thinking	Cognitive control
Neurotic versus stable self-representation	Tendency to interpret stressors as threatening or self-derived faults versus as external factors	Perception and understanding of self and others

Source: RDoC: Research Domain Criteria

patient's current behaviors. This exchange need not end in a review of an anxiety or cluster C personality disorder to be effective for the patient.

In addition to influencing the clinician's perception, using categorical labels stokes the patient's fears of stigmatization. Though social acceptance of mental illness has increased over time, many patients worry about discrimination from others as well as the self-alienation that comes from perceiving oneself as abnormal or defective. The implications of this worry are significant: perceived stigmatization is associated with decreases in help-seeking behavior and treatment adherence.[6] Explaining maladaptive patterns of cognition, problem solving, and interpersonal relatedness from a dimensional perspective allows the clinician to communicate the problem in a manner that the patient can hear without becoming immediately defensive, fearful, or ashamed.

Final Thoughts

This technique works well for patients whose problematic behaviors and thought processes were likely originally adaptive but have grown to become impairing, such as occurs with post-traumatic stress disorder or anxiety disorders. Some patients feel attacked when given a categorical diagnosis, especially a personality disorder. This technique engenders more understanding on the part of the clinician and less defensiveness on the part of the patient.

Notwithstanding the helpfulness of dimensional diagnosis in general, some patients do not respond well to its inherent ambiguity and find comfort in a definitive categorical diagnosis. Use an appreciation of the patient's comprehension and interaction style from prior encounters to guide the use of this technique. Tailor your approach to the patient and be flexible. It is okay to switch to a more categorical approach if a dimensional one is failing, or vice versa.

References

1. McHugh P. Classifying psychiatric disorders: an alternative approach. *Harv Ment Health Lett.* 2002;19(5):7–8.

2. Schroeder M, Wormworth J, Livesley W. Dimensions of personality disorder and their relationship to the big five dimensions of personality. *Psychol Assess*. 1992;4(1):47–53.

3. Cloninger RC. Temperament and personality. *Curr Opin Neurobiol*. 1994;4(2):266–267.

4. Karson M, Fox J. Common skills that underlie the common factors of successful psychotherapy. *Am J Psychother*. 2010;64(3):269–281.

5. Insel T, Cuthbert B, Garvey M, et al. Research domain criteria (RDoC): toward a new classification framework for research on mental disorders. *Am J Psychiatry*. 2010;167(7):748–751.

6. Kelly C, Jorm A. Stigma and mood disorders. *Curr Opin Psychiatry*. 2007;20(1):13–16.

36

Label the Patient's Affect

Help Manage the Patient's Emotional Experience by Putting It Into Words

EDWARD MacPHEE, MD

Setting

Emotions are experienced preverbally. Even before the patient is aware of their own intense feelings, clinicians may notice them through the patient's tone of voice (called paralanguage), body language (called kinesics), or choice of words. Strong emotions may become dysregulating and counterproductive if not managed during the patient encounter. For the patient to handle intense feelings, these emotions need to be put into words. The clinician can help with this process by helping the patient find the words for their own emotions through a technique called affect labeling.

The Technique

Notice the presence of the patient's emotions, particularly through their paralanguage and kinesics. When these emotions begin arising, help the patient label their own affect in three steps:

1. Have the patient relax with a behavioral coping skill for about 5–10 seconds.
2. Instruct the patient to create a sentence that starts with a word or phrase that captures the emotion and ends with a brief description of the situation. The sentence often looks like this:

   I feel *emotional word or phrase* because of *a brief description of the situation*.
   E.g., I feel *like I'm all alone now* because *my partner died*.

3. Ask the patient if there is anything they would like to add or modify about the statement.

Sample Dialogue

> Patient: Since I lost my job two weeks ago, I've been having a really difficult time.

Clinician: I hear from your tone of voice and see from your expression how this brings up a lot of strong emotions for you.

> Yes, it does.

Sometimes when a person is experiencing strong emotions, it's helpful to put them into words. Can we try this together?

> OK.

First, let's take a few moments to relax. Do you feel like you're ready?

> I am.

I'd like you to make a sentence that starts with a word or phrase that captures the emotion and ends with a brief description of why you're experiencing the emotions. An example would be "I'm feeling queasy because I don't know what the doctor is going to say about my tests." How does that sound?

> OK—I feel like I've let myself and my family down because I lost my job.

I understand. Is there anything you'd like to add or change about that statement?

> I'll add that I'm terrified now that I don't know what the future looks like.

Losing your job can certainly lead to these types of feelings.

Why This Works

The usefulness of putting one's feelings into words is not a new idea. The Dutch philosopher Baruch Spinoza commented in *Ethics* in 1677 that "emotion, which is suffering, ceases to be suffering as soon as we form a clear and precise picture of it."[1] Today, psychotherapists commonly help patients put their emotional experiences into words, and neuroscientific evidence supports the value of this approach. Whether in spoken or written form, naming emotions tempers the brain's responses to negative emotions by reducing amygdala activity and activating the prefrontal cortex, where more complex cognitive functions are seated.[2-4]

The two most common techniques to help patients label their emotions are empathy statements and affect labeling. An empathy statement is a statement in which the clinician notices the patient's emotions and presents their understanding of why the patient is feeling that way. For example, "I see how sad you are about what happened." The advantages of this approach are that it fits smoothly into the interview and that it demonstrates that the clinician cares about what the patient is experiencing. Empathy statements are invaluable for improving the therapeutic alliance. However, empathy statements can be challenging to do well and occasionally miss the mark—an event known as empathic failure. Empathic failure occurs when the clinician mis- or under-represents the patient's experience.

Affect labeling helps the clinician and patients manage emotions but carries little risk of empathic failure. Unlike empathy statements, affect labeling is led by the patient. In the sample dialogue, a brief moment of de-escalation introduces the therapeutic intervention, reinforces the patient's sense of agency and self-control, and thereby enables the patient to employ higher-order cognitive functions that had been obscured by emotional intensity. From this more composed moment, the clinician helps the patient label their emotional state and contextualize it among their recent stressors. The patient's implicit emotional experience becomes explicit and brings into the conscious, cognitive realm what had previously been preverbal and inaccessible. Once the patient's emotional information is available cognitively, its importance can be understood and used to inform choices. Affect labeling has its limitations. First, it requires more time to do well. Also, as a discrete therapeutic intervention, it interrupts the flow of the conversation more than do empathy statements.

Final Thoughts

Many people have difficulties putting their emotions into words, particularly when those emotions overwhelm one's ability to think critically and rationally. An inability to describe one's own emotions is called alexithymia; chronic alexithymia is seen among patients with severe depression, schizophrenia, developmental disabilities, and somatic symptom disorders.[5] But often patients who are overwhelmed and highly emotional have momentary difficulty describing their emotions, too. Affect labeling helps patients verbalize their emotions and serves as a useful adjunct to empathy statements.

References

1. Frankl VE. *Man's Search for Meaning: An Introduction to Logotherapy.* New York, NY: Simon & Schuster; 1984: 74.
2. Frattaroli J. Experimental disclosure and its moderators: a meta-analysis. *Psychol Bull.* 2005;132(6):823–865.

3. Pennebaker JW, Chung CK. Expressive writing: connections to physical and mental health. In: Friedman HS, ed. *The Oxford Handbook of Health Psychology*. New York, NY: Oxford University Press; 2011.

4. Lieberman MD, Eisenberger NI, Crockett MJ, Tom SM, Pfeifer JH, Way BM. Putting feelings into words: affect labeling disrupts amygdala activity to affective stimuli. *Psychol Sci.* 2007;18(5):421–428.

5. Samur D, Tops M, Schlinkert C, Quirin M, Cuijpers P, Koole SL. Four decades of research on alexithymia: moving toward clinical applications. *Front Psychol.* 2013;4;1–4.

37

Talk About the Mind-Body Connection
Connect Psychiatric and Medical Symptoms to Encourage Openness to Mental Health Interventions

THIDA THANT, MD

Setting

Patients' psychiatric symptoms significantly impact their medical illness. However, many patients are more comfortable discussing their physical symptoms: many patients with major depression do not perceive the need for, or want, mental health treatment.[1] Patients overly focused on physical symptoms at the exclusion of psychiatric ones often need help to reflect on how emotions and mood, worries and fears are exacerbating their medical recovery. Helping patients make this connection improves medical outcomes and clinical interactions.[2]

The Technique

Clinicians must inform the patient of the link between the mind and body and how each affects the other. Although this discussion may feel uncomfortable for the clinician and unfamiliar to the patient, several strategies help clinicians provide effective psychoeducation. Discuss psychological symptoms as matter-of-factly as you would discuss medical symptoms. Use approachable examples—such as how stress and anxiety can cause stomach upset, headaches, or muscle tension. Avoid technical terms such as "depression" or "anxiety" in favor of more colloquial terms such as "frustration," "stress," "feeling down," or "worries."

Sample Dialogue

Clinician: I see that you mentioned on this form that you have been feeling depressed lately?

Patient: I have lots of back pain; I don't have anything like depression.

> Do you have any worries about your pain or ever feel frustrated by having to deal with pain?

> Sure, I'm in pain! But if my pain was gone then everything would be fine.

> Well, we know that the mind and body are linked, so what affects one affects the other. If we treat both your body as well as find ways to cope with worries you are having, your pain may improve.

> What do you mean the mind and body are linked?

> For example, when people feel worried or stressed, they may notice that they get "butterflies" in their stomach, or that their muscles get tense, or that they have headaches.

Why This Works

Psychoeducation is the process of providing education and information about mental health symptoms or disorders to patients and family members. Helping patients connect the impact of their emotions to their physical health through psychoeducation is a critical component of medical care.

Patients who are overly focused on somatic symptoms often feel defensive, resistant, or hurt when asked about psychiatric symptoms in the context of a visit for physical symptoms. If the topic is approached poorly, patients may feel invalidated ("Doctors never listen to me."), judged ("Are you saying it's all in my head?"), or abandoned by the medical system. This reaction may lead to doctor shopping or avoidance of medical care entirely. However, when physicians are informative and respectful, patients grow more committed to treatment regimens and experience better health.[2]

This technique mitigates patient resistance to discussion of the mind-body connection through rapport building (using validation and listening), development of a common language (by using terms favored by the patient), and destigmatization (through delivering psychoeducation). If met with defensiveness or anger, the clinician should validate the patient's frustrations and then gently remind them that clinicians are not here to place judgment or determine what is a true physical symptom. Rather, clinicians seek to provide well-rounded, holistic care that helps the patient achieve their goals. It can be helpful to describe mental health interventions as simply another "tool in the toolbox" of treatment alongside exercise, good nutrition, and medications.

Active listening and patient-centered statements are key components of this technique. Active listening is a communication style that involves being able to fully concentrate on, recognize, and explore what is being said by patients.[3] The use of active listening allows the clinician to pick up on subtle clues patients may share as to what they believe is causing their symptoms, what would be helpful, and what is worrying them. These clues include frequent referencing of a word, intense focus on particular symptoms, or reluctance to accept recommendations. The clinician then explores these clues to build rapport, obtain more information, and begin treatment. Patient-centered statements elicit elaboration from a patient and encourage collaboration: "What do you think is going on? What do you think would be most helpful? Together we can work on a treatment plan that could help." Once you have successfully utilized this technique, it becomes easier to discuss recommendations for mental health treatment and help patients engage with psychiatric clinicians.

Final Thoughts

This technique reflects the importance of listening to patients, meeting them wherever they are emotionally, and developing a common language with which to communicate. This technique is especially helpful in hospital or integrated care settings where patients are more typically presenting for medical care. Consider using this technique when the patient and their clinician have different ideas as to the cause of symptoms or the importance of mental healthcare. Being comfortable discussing the mind-body connection is helpful for both mental health and medical clinicians to decrease clinician burnout and improve patient satisfaction.[2]

References

1. Williams JW. Competing demands: does care for depression fit in primary care? *J Gen Intern Med*. 1998;13(2):137–139.
2. Street R, Gordon H, Haidet P. Physicians' communication and perceptions of patients: is it how they look, how they talk, or is it just the doctor? *Soc Sci Med*. 2007;65(3):586–598.
3. Lang F. Clues to patients' explanations and concerns about their illnesses: a call for active listening. *Arch Fam Med*. 2000;9(3):222–227.

38

Emphasize Function Over Feeling in Chronic Illness

Shift the Visit's Focus to Capability to Reinforce the Patient's Self-Efficacy and Agree on Achievable Outcomes

Setting

Co-morbidity is common among patients in all medical settings. The simultaneous presence of multiple medical and psychiatric symptoms often leaves clinicians feeling uncertain where to start in treatment. Particularly difficult to manage are patients with chronic pain or psychiatric illness, who frequently have multiple diagnoses. Clinicians feel overwhelmed trying to address all these concerns in a coherent treatment strategy. Eventually both clinicians and patients grow tired of the seeming lack of symptom resolution.

The Technique

For patients with multiple chronic somatic and psychiatric complaints, emphasize the patient's functioning over symptom control. Start by validating the patient's concerns through obtaining more detail on their pain, mood, and other symptoms. Then transition to a discussion around how they are functioning—for example, Are they meeting their responsibilities at home and work?—and what they would be doing if these symptoms were controlled. The success of treatment should be evaluated through progress towards these behavioral goals rather than amelioration of symptoms.

Sample Dialogue

Patient: But I just haven't been able to keep up with housework since my back has been hurting so much more.

Clinician: What has your back pain felt like over this past week?

> Well, you know, I always have that dull throbbing, but now it feels like there's a heavy sensation on the left side. That's new. And then I need to lay down and that doesn't help much.

> You mentioned keeping up with housework. If your pain were better controlled, what would you be doing that you're not now?

> I always feel so good when the yard is mowed and cleaned up, and the kitchen is tidy. When I'm in pain, I don't keep up with those things, the house starts looking like a mess, and I feel really guilty.

Why This Works

Chronic somatic conditions such as pain and polysymptomatology are among the most difficult conditions for clinicians to treat. Once an urgent diagnosis has been excluded, clinicians often feel they are playing whack-a-mole trying to address the frequency or quality of the patient's symptoms. Ultimately, this game is futile, because many patients who have chronic pain are likely to go on experiencing some aberrant sensations indefinitely. Worse, the pursuit of resolving all averse somatic experiences has led to iatrogenic harm such as through the over-prescription of opioid medication.

The presence of multiple symptoms itself warrants unique diagnostic considerations. The manner in which symptoms are solicited makes a difference; patients report a greater number of somatic symptoms on questionnaires than when speaking directly to a clinician.[1] Somatic symptom disorders are familiar to many clinicians, however, patients with certain psychiatric disorders (particularly cluster B personality disorders and post-traumatic pathology) endorse similar rates of somatic symptoms.[2]

A more productive and rewarding approach is to orient the history and treatment around the patient's functioning.[3] Pain is the perception of tissue damage—a perception that is inaccurate among many patients whose pain has become chronic. For these patients there may be no underlying tissue damage, and pain is a complex phenomenon representing abnormalities of neurologic transmission, sensation sensitivity, and cognitive distortions around the meaning of pain. The treatment approach must be accordingly more complex and incorporate non-pharmacologic and physical therapies and occupational rehabilitation.

Refocusing the interview on function provides achievable, concrete treatment goals whose achievement the clinician can witness alongside their patient (unlike the sensation of pain that is knowable only to the patient). This technique reinforces the patient's sense of self-efficacy, itself an important component of eventual rehabilitation.[4] Thus the clinician should emphasize the importance of functioning in improving symptoms (rather than vice versa).

Final Thoughts

To proceed directly to a focus on functioning will typically and rightfully be perceived as invalidating by the patient. Many patients with chronic somatic pains have grown frustrated as being dismissed by clinicians who do not take their pain seriously. As in the sample dialogue, the clinician should take some time to elicit the patient's characterization of pain. While it is important to exclude urgent pathology, the more important reason for obtaining this history is to understand and validate the patient's experience. But having received this history, the clinician should move on to understand and emphasize the patient's functional goals. This technique works well with patients who have fairly distinct (if polymorphous) co-morbidities; patients with multiple concurrent medical, psychiatric, and social stressors might benefit more from the technique described in chapter 47, "Imagine the Future."

References

1. Iverson GL, Brooks BL, Ashton VL, Lange RT. Interview versus questionnaire symptom reporting in people with the postconcussion syndrome. *J Head Trauma Rehabil.* 2010;25(1):23–30.
2. Lenze EJ, Miller AR, Munir ZB, Pornnoppadol C, North CS. Psychiatric symptoms endorsed by somatization disorder patients in a psychiatric clinic. *Ann Clin Psychiatry.* 1999;11(2):73–79.
3. Pavlinich M, Perret D, Rivers WE, et al. Physiatry, pain management and the opioid crisis: a focus on function. *Am J Phys Med Rehabil.* 2018;97(11):856–860.
4. Jackson T, Wang Y, Wang Y, Fan H. Self-efficacy and chronic pain outcomes: a meta-analytic review. *J Pain.* 2014;15(8):800–814.

39

Consider the Social History in Your Assessment

Apply the Social History as a Tool for Understanding the Patient's Diagnosis and Treatment

JODI ZIK, MD

Setting

To obtain the most information during a time-limited session, clinicians are often tempted to gloss over a patient's social history in favor of other questions thought to be more pertinent. Doing so is a mistake. A good social history provides valuable insight into the context of the patient's illness and is invaluable for guiding effective treatment. The context provided by social history significantly impacts care, especially when working among diverse patient populations or with unexpected challenges in treatment.

The Technique

When setbacks arise, ask questions about the patient's social history to better understand obstacles in treatment. A detailed social history might include information about the patient's living situation, relationship and family dynamics, religion, sexual history, drug and alcohol use, educational attainment, and culture. Better understanding the patient's background requires you not only to educate yourself about their culture but also to allow the patient to teach you about their personal perspective.

Sample Dialogue

> Clinician: It seems you've had more difficulty maintaining normal blood pressures lately.

> Patient: Life at home is a bit crazy now. I'm doing everything I can.

> Tell me a little bit about what your home life looks like.

> Well, I'm Hispanic. In our culture, we care for our elders. So I live with my *abuela*, my parents, two of my aunts, three of my cousins, my husband, and my children.

That's quite a full house. And what are your responsibilities?

> Well, I give everyone their medications and then need to take my own. It's been harder since my father moved in. He abused me when I was a child. I feel like I'm always on edge. I can't sleep at night.

Thank you for sharing some of your story with me. With all of these things going on, I imagine it's easy to miss taking your medication.

> I know what you tell me is always for my own good, and I didn't want to say anything, but there are days I just can't remember if I've taken the medication or not.

I'm glad you told me! It sounds like there's a lot going on. I wonder if a pill box will help you remember whether you've taken your medication. We should also talk about how I can support you in managing the emotional issues from your trauma that you just raised.

Why This Works

Social epidemiology is the study of how a person's environment affects physical and psychological health.[1] Sociocultural factors, including community-level factors, influence health in significant ways. For example, medication adherence, blood sugar testing, and cholesterol of patients with diabetes have significant relationships with neighborhood factors including food insecurity, social support, and neighborhood violence.[2] Forgoing social history leads the clinician to miss important elements influencing the patient, their health, their interactions with the clinician, and their approach to treatment.

The significance and integration of the social history into treatment planning is too often neglected. Clinicians may feel that social factors are unchangeable or that the time pressures of a clinical interview do not allow for exploration of these factors,[3,4] but skimming over social factors decreases the effectiveness of care. When a patient's treatment is not going according to plan, consider whether their social environment has changed. The social history also aids preventive care by uncovering potential health risks or ongoing, unresolved issues. For example, a patient's sexual habits may put them at risk for sexually transmitted diseases, or their financial limitations may complicate adherence.

In the sample dialogue, the clinician raises concerns about the patient's uncontrolled blood pressure. The patient alludes to issues at home, and the clinician used this opportunity to seek more information about the patient's home life. Several psychological and logistical challenges quickly became apparent. First, the patient's responsibilities at home are interfering with their ability to regularly take medication. In addition, the patient's history is suspicious for post-traumatic stress disorder—a condition that poses increased risk for complications of cardiac illness.[5] Finally, the patient's culture may have prevented the clinician from discovering this history absent direct inquiry. Hispanic culture values the concept of "simpatía," or "kindness," in which persons navigate away from conflict even when faced with obstacles.[6] Thus, the social history provided a wealth of social and cultural information for problem-solving this patient's treatment.

Although medical education has begun to incorporate diversity in healthcare into training, social factors are frequently neglected in cross-cultural education.[7] This communication gap between patients and clinicians leads to sub-optimal care. By taking a little extra time to understand a patient and their social factors, later confusion over key factors in a patient's health can be avoided.

Final Thoughts

This technique can be used with all patients and is particularly helpful when working with patients from cultural backgrounds less familiar to the clinician. Sociocultural factors directly and indirectly influence the patient's health and disease course; the clinician should emphasize social history in the interview to understand these factors. Further, asking specific questions about the patient's social history avoids the risk of the clinician making broad assumptions about an individual based on heritage or socioeconomic status. Exploration of social history yields accurate, contextualized, and helpful information that improves the patient's care.

References

1. Macintyre S, Ellaway A. Ecological approaches: rediscovering the role of the physical and social environment. In: Berkman LF, Kawachi I, eds. *Social Epidemiology*. New York, NY: Oxford University Press; 2000:332–348.
2. Smalls BL, Gregory CM, Zoller JS, Egede LE. Assessing the relationship between neighborhood factors and diabetes related health outcomes and self-care behaviors. *BMC Health Serv Res.* 2015;15:445.
3. Fleegler EW, Lieu TA, Wise PH, Muret-Wagstaff S. Families' health-related social problems and missed referral opportunities. *Pediatrics.* 2007;119(6):e1332–1341.
4. Kenyon C, Sandel M, Silverstein M, Skair A, Zuckerman B. Revisiting the social history for child health. *Pediatrics.* 2007;120(3):e734–e738.
5. Levine AB, Levine LM, Levin TB. Posttraumatic stress disorder and cardiometabolic disease. *Cardiology.* 2014;127(1):1–19.
6. Juckett G. Caring for Latino patients. *Am Fam Physician.* 2013;87(1):48–54.
7. Green AR, Betancourt JR, Carrillo JE. Integrating social factors into cross-cultural medical education. *Acad Med.* 2002;77(3):193–197.

40

Remind the Patient What Is Not Working

Ask How the Patient Feels About Their Current Behaviors in Order to Motivate Change

Setting

Despite the fact that they keep returning for care, sometimes it feels like patients are stuck. Stuck in unhealthy habits, unhelpful routines, and an abeyance of progress. The clinician might try to discuss the risks and benefits of behavior change only to find this approach is not as impactful as hoped. Every appointment feels like the same problem. This technique offers a way to non-judgmentally reflect on the patient's lack of treatment progress and thereby motivate changes in behavior.

The Technique

When patients are expressing doubt or unwillingness to change current behaviors, ask how well their current habits are working for them. The answer is probably, "Not well." The purpose of asking is not to obtain this corroborating answer so much as help the patient refocus on their goals and how their current behavior is not achieving those goals. The question should be posed in a non-judgmental manner. Discuss with the patient why they came to see you and how changing their behavior, though difficult, will ultimately result in better outcomes.

Sample Dialogue

Clinician: How have you been doing since our last appointment?

Patient: I don't know, trying to just get out of the house has been pretty difficult, let alone going back to work. I haven't done much. I just don't feel motivated.

> That does not sound like things are going well, and we've been talking about being more active for a while now. Do you feel like what you are doing now is working for you?

> It's not working at all. I still feel bad all the time.

> Since just staying in the house isn't helping you feel better, we need to do something differently or else it's unlikely you will feel differently. You're coming to appointments—which suggests to me you want to do something about how you're feeling.

> That makes sense. Whatever I'm doing know isn't helping, and of course I'd rather feel better.

> Great! Let's talk about specifics.

Why This Works

Patients make and keep medical appointments for a reason. There is something happening in their life that they want to be different, even if the clinician sometimes feels like progress is not happening.

In asking the patient how their current behavior is working, clinicians frame change from the patient's perspective. Something about the patient's current behavior is not working, or else the patient would not be seeking assistance. This fact is so straightforward that it is easy to forget! That the patient is coming in for an appointment is evidence of their commitment to change. Nonetheless, big changes are more likely to elicit resistance from the patient, so the clinician needs a strategy to help the patient consider the relative risks of doing nothing, that is, avoiding change.

This technique reflects lessons from behavioral activation therapy, an evidence-based treatment for depression and other disorders.[1] Behavioral activation has been adapted into brief forms that help patients pursue regular activities consistent with their goals for treatment and values in life.[2] A succinct summary of this psychotherapeutic approach is, "If you do nothing, nothing will change." Alongside helping the patient develop a behavioral plan, the clinician continually reinforces the patient's motivation to change. Ways to cultivate that motivation include explicitly calling out the patient's dissatisfaction with how things are going and also the positive steps they have taken towards change, including coming to appointments. In the sample dialogue, the patient may feel overwhelmed at the prospect of leaving the house, but their concerns at this prospect are contextualized with their frustration at how poorly things are going right now. When the status quo becomes entrenched, the clinician must help the patient recognize how doing nothing and continuing on the same course will not achieve the patient's goals.

Final Thoughts

Behavioral change is difficult. Some patients are unable to admit that their current behaviors are not serving them. This lack of insight can be particularly challenging with patients who have substance use disorders and are stubbornly unready to enact behavioral change. In using this technique, the clinician may generate some helpful ambivalence in the patient around whether change is worthwhile; other techniques useful managing ambivalence about change are described in chapters 51 and 57.

References

1. Sturmey P. Behavioral activation is an evidence-based treatment for depression. *Behav Modif.* 2009;33(6):818–829.
2. Balan IC, Lejuez CW, Hoffer M, Blanco C. Integrating motivational interviewing and brief behavioral activation therapy: theoretical and practical considerations. *Cogn Behav Pract.* 2016;23(2):205–220.

41

Ask About Medication Side Effects

Assess Experiences of Side Effects When Medications Are Seemingly Ineffective

VIVIAN CHENG, PHARMD, AND
JEFFREY CLARK, PHARMD, BCPP

Setting

Clinicians are prescribing more medications than ever. The percentage of Americans prescribed three or more drugs is now 22%—an increase from only 12% about 20 years ago.[1] But in the words of former U.S. Surgeon General C. Everett Koop, "Drugs don't work in patients who don't take them." When medications appear to be ineffective, clinicians should consider medication adherence with patients before changing treatment regimens.

The Technique

Ask the patient if they have noticed any potential side effects related to medication use. Ask, "What potential side effects are you concerned about with your medications?" When patients endorse non-adherence, refrain from the scold-and-scare tactic. Instead be empathetic: thank the patient for their honesty and emphasize that you will work together to face challenges and achieve mutually set goals. Discuss with the patient how they might improve adherence and focus on the feasibility of any proposed plans by asking if the plan is something "you will do" rather than if "you can do" it.

Sample Dialogue

Patient: I don't know if my medication is working; my blood pressure still seems really high.

Clinician: Let's talk about what's going on. What potential side effects are you concerned about with your new medication?

Actually, I started having pretty bad headaches. To be honest, I stopped taking the medication after a few days.

I'm sorry that happened, and I'm glad you told me. Let's talk about your headaches. Headaches are a common side effect but usually go away after about a week as your body adjusts to the medication. What are your thoughts about trying this medication again but giving your body more time?

I didn't realize that could happen. I guess it's worth another shot.

Is this something you'll do?

Why This Works

Medication-taking behavior is complex. When asked directly, patients might not accurately portray their medication adherence. There are several reasons for patients' inaccurate reporting. Many patients want to please their clinician and therefore say what they believe the clinician wants to hear. Also, patients may feel it is easier to endorse medication adherence than discuss why they are not taking medications as instructed. Other patients practice "white coat adherence" and take medications only for a short period of time in preparation for their visit.

Asking about side effects affords the patient an opportunity to discuss their concerns about medications in a manner that invites discussion of the patient's experience. Use of the word "potential" invites the patient to broadly discuss any concurrent symptoms regardless of how closely connected they may actually be to the medication. The clinician's job is to assess whether those symptoms are truly associated with the medication.

This technique also normalizes the possibility of non-adherence and thereby invites the patient to raise other concerns including cost, complexity of administration, or other barriers.[3] Avoiding accusatory language or tone reduces pressure on the patient to misrepresent adherence in hopes of being a "good patient." In a strong clinical relationship, the clinician and patient explore the causes of non-adherence together. Such a relationship is built through the clinician's active demonstration of empathy and the presence of a comfortable environment for the patient to be honest about medication-taking behavior.

The discussion should end by anticipating with the patient any challenges to adherence. The patient's misconceptions, questions, and concerns should be addressed immediately to improve both adherence and also the clinician-patient relationship. But ultimately only the patient is the one who will decide to take any medication. Using the phrase "will you" returns responsibility for adherence to the patient. This phrase makes the idea of taking medication more real and helps the patient visualize how likely they are to actually take the medication. In imagining the future so concretely, additional barriers to adherence often become apparent. As with medications, adherence strategies are meaningless if the patient will not use them!

Final Thoughts

The clinician's first thought when medications are ineffective should not be to add another medication. Instead consider whether the patient is adherent with medications that are prescribed. Roughly 3% to 10% of total U.S. healthcare costs—up to $300 billion annually—are due to medication non-adherence.[4] About 20%–30% of prescriptions are never filled, and 50% of medications for chronic diseases are not taken as prescribed.[5,6] Patients have many different reasons for not taking medications and still more reasons for not being straightforward in reporting adherence. Clinicians should start the discussion around adherence in a non-accusatory, open-ended manner that invites the patient's collaboration.

References

1. National Center for Health Statistics. *Health, United States, 2017: With Special Feature on Mortality*. Hyattsville, MD: U.S. Department of Health and Human Services; 2018.
2. Osterberg L, Blaschke T. Adherence to medication. *N Engl J Med*. 2005;353(5):487–497.
3. Hugtenburg JG, Timmers L, Elders PJ, Verloet M, van Dijk L. Definitions, variants, and causes of nonadherence with medication: a challenge for tailored inventions. *Patient Prefer Adherence*. 2013;7:675–682.
4. New England Healthcare Institute. *Thinking Outside the Pillbox: A System-wide Approach to Improving Patient Medication Adherence for Chronic Disease*. Cambridge, MA: New England Healthcare Institute; 2009.
5. Peterson AM, Takiya L, Finley R. Meta-analysis of trials of interventions to improve medication adherence. *Am J Health Syst Pharm*. 2003;60(7):657–665.
6. World Health Organization. *The World Health Report 2002: Reducing Risks, Promoting Healthy Life*. Geneva, Switzerland: World Health Organization; 2002.

42

Ask the "Why" About Online Information

Focus on the Patient's Motivations for Sharing Information Brought to the Encounter

Setting

Most patients seek information about their symptoms and medical illness online, even if they do not discuss the information during a clinical encounter.[1,2] Patients may be resistant to discuss their findings due to embarrassment, fear, or concern for challenging the traditional expertise of the clinician.[3] Clinicians often worry about patients bringing material out of concern that they will appear dismissive towards the patient's interests or unknowledgeable should the patient ask about novel treatments unknown to the clinician. Clinicians must be prepared to have a discussion with patients about the information they bring to the encounter.

The Technique

Ask the patient to talk about the information they found and focus on why they were searching for that information. These answers will be more revealing as to the patient's health literacy, concerns, and treatment goals than a discussion of the discovered content itself. Let the patient hold any printed materials themselves and assume the role of teacher. If the patient has brought in grossly erroneous information, offer corrections and perspective. Patients should be encouraged to use websites free of commercial bias and material published by reputable universities and health agencies.

Sample Dialogue

> Patient: I was reading online about my hypertension, and I actually brought this printout.

> Clinician: Of course, thank you for bringing this in. Show me what you have, and tell me about what you found.

So it's a lot of stuff, and I don't know how much of it I believe. Here it starts talking a little about the side effects of the medication; these were really scary. Maybe I'm better off not taking it.

Sure, let's talk about that. What led you to look up this information online?

Well, doesn't everybody do that? It was just really scary for me to hear how high my blood pressure was at our last visit. You know, my father had hypertension and then had a stroke, so I really wanted to understand how I can get better.

Why This Works

By definition, patients have less knowledge of the science behind their illness, and it is the clinician's duty to use their own knowledge in the patient's service.[4] Unfortunately, poor information about medical illnesses abounds on the internet.[5] Clinicians typically feel comfortable talking about the facts of illnesses and treatments, and the patient's search for material online prior to the visit need not complicate this precedent. Patients' bringing information to the appointment is not a sign of distrust in any individual or the profession as much as a desire to prepare for a more collaborative, productive clinical encounter. In fact, patients who search for information online about their symptoms appear to enjoy stronger therapeutic relationships with their clinicians.[1]

Facts found online are easily reconciled with the clinician's knowledge. Yet this technique encourages a broader exploration of the patient's relationship with their online searching. The sample dialogue demonstrates the clinician letting the patient play the role of teacher. The patient expounds on what they found and thereby helps the clinician understand what is most important about these materials for the patient. This patient immediately betrays some sense of perspective: the online materials are somewhat overwhelming and lack the credibility to supplant the clinician's opinion. It appears the patient is considering starting a medication. When the clinician asks the patient to further explain their motivation for researching this illness, a more substantial fear becomes apparent.

Understanding the patient's relationship to their online search provides insight for the clinician's own instruction and treatment planning. This patient appears eager to learn and appropriately skeptical; they may appreciate a more nuanced discussion of treatment options. That side effects were a prominent concern may affect adherence and medication selection. This patient may be motivated to pursue non-pharmacologic treatments for hypertension if indicated. And the patient's family history may be a factor in diagnosis and treatment—Might this patient have white coat hypertension?[6]—or anticipate future complications including anxiety.

Psychotherapists often mind the difference between content and process. Content describes the facts of the visit. For example, this patient is talking about information that they found online. Process describes the unspoken, even unconscious work that happens concurrently with the content. Process is somewhat amorphous and far more interesting. What is the process in this exchange? If the clinician merely addressed the facts that the patient found online, there would seem to be little deepening of the clinical relationship. Perhaps the clinician would be proud of themselves for having demonstrated their knowledge. But through using this technique instead, the clinician deepened the therapeutic relationship by gaining greater insight into the patient's perspective, raising important concerns, and allying with the patient in a process of diagnosis and treatment. The clinician changes the clinician-patient relationship. The clinician is not simply the teacher and the patient a student. Rather, both the clinician and patient share some mastery of the subject and collaborate in a shared task, whether considering information found online or fighting disease. That change and strengthening of the therapeutic relationship represents the process underlying this encounter.

Final Thoughts

This technique allows clinicians to take an inviting and inquisitive approach to the patient's bringing in health information from an external source. Whereas most patients bring in the results of online medical searches, other patients bring in materials like political or personal paraphernalia of little relevance to medical treatment. This technique can be applied for such non-medical information as well. Admittedly, these episodes are enlightening and potentially comical as to how the patient envisions the clinical relationship. The clinician must be careful not to violate professional boundaries including by being overly familiar or self-disclosing. Discussing the patient's reasons for bringing those materials is a nice transition towards other topics of greater import.

References

1. Cocco AM, Zordan R, Taylor DM, et al. Dr Google in the ED: searching for online health information by adult emergency department patients. *Med J Aust.* 2018;209(8):342–347.
2. Waring ME, McManus DD, Amante DJ, Darling CE, Kiefe CI. Online health information seeking by adults hospitalized for acute coronary syndromes: who looks for information, and who discusses it with healthcare providers? *Patient Educ Couns.* 2018;101(11):1973–1981.
3. Tan SS, Goonawardene N. Internet health information seeking and the patient-physician relationship: a systematic review. *J Med Internet Res.* 2017;19(1):e9.
4. Haupt CE. Professional ethics, personal conscience, and public expectations. *J Clin Ethics.* 2016;27(3):233–237.
5. Hirsch M, Aggarwal S, Barker C, Davis CJ, Duffy JMN. Googling endometriosis: a systematic review of information available on the internet. *Am J Obstet Gynecol.* 2017;216(5):451–458.e1.
6. Martin CA, McGrath BP. White-coat hypertension. *Clin Exp Pharmacol Physiol.* 2014;41(1): 22–29.

43

Recall the Patient's Strengths

Consider How the Patient's Abilities Can Be Used in the Service of Their Health

Setting

Hope and motivation are traits that vary among patients and over time. Some patients feel more hopeful the easier the treatment is perceived to be. For others, hope and motivation are relatively fixed, regardless of whether they perceive treatment to be easy or difficult.[1] Hopelessness and low motivation limit patients' ability to engage in treatment; hopelessness in particular is correlated with worse life functioning.[2] Yet even patients with low hope and motivation have had success in overcoming obstacles in their past. Discovering the strengths that fueled these past successes should be leveraged in the current moment.

The Technique

When a patient expresses doubts that they can adhere to treatment or that the treatment will work, consider with the patient similar challenges they have faced in the past. Ask the patient the specifics of the past situation, focusing on how the situation may have seemed insurmountable at first, though, in the end, the patient persevered and perhaps thrived. Then draw a parallel to the present situation and invite the patient to consider how their prior strengths can be applied to the current treatment plan.

Sample Dialogue

Patient: I don't know. I don't think I'll be able to take this medicine every day, and I don't think it will help even if I do.

Clinician: I hear you: it does sound like a big change. When's the last time you had to make a big change in your life?

> Well, I remember when we moved across town. My commute got a lot longer, and I couldn't take the train anymore. I am not a morning person, and I wasn't sure if it was going to work out. But now I like my job and my new house, now it's been good.

That sounds like a huge adjustment, and you were able to make it work. It sounds like you were persistent and determined. Do you ever feel like it wasn't worth moving?

> At first I did. But now I'm used to the commute, I enjoy listening to music in the car and seeing my friends at work.

So that was difficult at first, but you stuck with it, and things worked out well. I wonder how this treatment might be a similar situation.

Why This Works

Clinicians are often energetic and hopeful persons, and they struggle to connect with patients who feel doubtful, hopeless, or unmotivated. Depressed patients in particular are prone to negative thought distortions in which they over-emphasize feelings of worthlessness and inefficacy. However, all patients have had the success of overcoming past obstacles, from small successes in work and life to surviving profound traumas. Helping the patient recall these successes is useful for generating hope that they will be able to overcome current challenges.

Recapturing the sense of prior successes enhances the patient's confidence and motivation. Even when the current treatment difficulties are likely to be different than difficulties faced in the past, the patient's feelings of hopelessness or doubt are probably similar. The patient's giving voice to their own prior success instills a sense of capability and purpose to their current efforts. When patients are struggling, they fail to give themselves credit for their strengths. Even relatively unremarkable successes—for example, adjusting to a new routine—can serve as reminders of personal strength and adaptability. This further enhances the patient's confidence in themselves as they approach the treatment plan.

All patients bring strengths to the clinical relationship—perhaps they are smart, perseverant, reliable, or kind. Perhaps they are generous or thoughtful. (Clinicians likewise bring their own unique strengths.) In the midst of illness, however, it is easy to neglect these strengths and harbor doubt, fear, distrust, and pessimism. Recovering one's health requires one to leverage these positive attributes. Many psychotherapists recognize the importance of encouraging patients' positive qualities, and cultivating patients' strengths is a core precept of many psychotherapeutic models including supportive psychotherapy and positive psychiatry.[3,4]

Final Thoughts

Rarely is the patient's hopelessness well-founded. Patients who are unable to reflect on any past successes as worthy of examination may be struggling with additional psychopathology such as a depressive or personality disorders. Patients who cannot partner in this technique may be more likely to benefit from other approaches that actively encourage participation in treatment, such as the techniques described in chapters 40 and 44. Most often patients are amenable to the clinician's brief efforts to reflect on past successes and quickly re-discover their hope and motivation for future successes.

References

1. Valtonen HM, Suominen K, Haukka J, et al. Hopelessness across phases of bipolar I or II disorder: a prospective study. *J Affect Disord*. 2009;115(1–2):11–17.
2. Morris CD, Miklowitz DJ, Wisniewski SR, Giese AA, Thomas MR, Allen MH. Care satisfaction, hope, and life functioning among adults with bipolar disorder: data from the first 1000 participants in the Systematic Treatment Enhancement Program. *Compr Psychiatry*. 2005;46(2):98–104.
3. Winston A, Rosenthal RN, Pinsker H. *Introduction to Supportive Psychotherapy*. 1st edition. Arlington, VA: American Psychiatric Publishing; 2004.
4. Summers RF, Jeste DV, eds. *Positive Psychiatry: A Casebook*. 1st edition. Arlington, VA: American Psychiatric Publishing; 2018.

44

Accept or Change

Simplify the Possible Outcomes to Help the Patient Stop Venting and Decide on Action

Setting

Patients sometimes spend appointment time voicing their frustrations. While venting brings relief if focused and occasional, unrestricted venting introduces a sense of frustration and helplessness to the clinical encounter. Clinicians feel overwhelmed and unable to refocus on more productive topics. One option for refocusing the interview is by posing a simple dichotomy for the patient that validates their frustration and challenges them to take ownership of their care: accept or change.

The Technique

When the patient presents with a complicated concern that appears to have no clear solution, validate their predicament. The situation might involve ambivalence over behavioral change, exasperation over life circumstances, or impatience with the pace of treatment. Summarize the patient's two possible choices: they can either accept the situation as it is and move on or do something to change the situation. Accepting the situation does not signify that the patient likes the situation. Nor does acceptance of the situation preclude choosing to change in the future. Rather, acceptance is the process of acknowledging the current situation as reality and making the decision to move on with life while tolerating the situation. On the other hand, the patient can elect to change their circumstances by creating and committing to a concrete plan of action.

Sample Dialogue

Patient: I can't believe they won't operate until my blood sugars are under better control: it's unfair! Can't they see how much pain I'm in! Nobody understands how hard my life is.

Clinician: I'm sorry that appointment didn't go as you had hoped, I know you want to have that procedure.

I do! And now I have to wait for who knows how long until my blood sugars miraculously improve, just so I can feel better. I'll just stop with my insulin then. Nothing matters. And no one cares!

I see two options here. We can accept that this is how it is right now, that the surgeons won't operate until your blood sugars improve. Then we'll move on to other ways to help you feel more comfortable. The other option is that we can decide to change what we can change, specifically focus on lowering your blood sugars and meeting the criteria for surgery.

Why This Works

Out of exasperation or a sense of unfairness, some patients come to the appointment venting and complaining without committing to treatment. The clinician cannot help but grow similarly frustrated—with the patient! This dynamic is a threat to the effectiveness of the therapeutic alliance. This technique helps the clinician move the clinical conversation from complaining to solution-generating. Dialectical behavior therapy, a psychotherapy designed for patients with borderline personality disorder, introduces the concept of radical acceptance.[1] Radical acceptance entails the patient's complete and total acceptance of a situation without judgment. Radical acceptance is predicated on the idea that not accepting reality perpetuates negative emotional states and keeps the patient stuck, wishing that the situation were different yet not doing anything to change their circumstances. Instead, when practicing radical acceptance, the patient accepts reality as it is and can decide what, if anything, they want to do about their current circumstances.

In this technique, the concepts of acceptance and change are viewed as dichotomous, mutually exclusive choices. The patient can do nothing or do something. Framing this choice forces the patient to accept greater ownership in the treatment relationship. In the sample dialogue, the patient exclaims that nobody cares and nobody is helping—the clinician present likely disagrees—while apparently abrogating their own responsibility for medication adherence. The patient and clinician are probably irritated with one another. The clinician needs to figure out a way through this impasse. The solution is to guide the patient to make a commitment one way or another: to agree to make a change in treatment, or to tolerate the current reality, however upsetting it may be. Even if the patient decides not to make a change, acceptance is typically sufficient to stem ruminative complaints about the unfairness of the situation. If the patient elects to change, the act of committing to this choice enhances motivation to enact that change.[2,3]

Interestingly, the frustrated clinician has the same choice as the patient: accept the encounter as it is or insert yourself to change the dynamic of the encounter. This technique helps the clinician resolve the patient's ambivalence and introduce some degree of confidence in treatment planning, regardless of whether the patients elects acceptance or change. Clinicians who are growing impatient with a venting patient will find that this technique facilitates the flow of the encounter and advances treatment.

This technique will not work if the clinician has not sufficiently validated the patient's perspective and challenges. The patient should feel heard and understood lest this technique be perceived as dismissive or even accusatory. Even when applying this technique, the clinician in the sample dialogue continues to interject brief validating statements. (Some examples of how to validate authentically and quickly are described in chapter 2.)

Final Thoughts

Patients bring many issues to appointments; sometimes these issues do not even relate to the initial reason for the visit. Clinicians can grow impatient and helpless in the absence of tools to refocus the patient's energy on more productive treatment goals. The successful therapeutic relationship is a partnership in which the clinician and patient share ownership for treatment. Unproductive venting can be therapeutic in bursts but left uncorralled will sap the energy of the relationship. This technique is a reminder that the clinician need not acquiesce to an unproductive status quo: they have the opportunity to help the patient choose how to proceed. Achieving clarity around the way forward resolves much of the pressure that underlies both parties' frustrations.

References

1. Linehan M. *Cognitive-Behavioral Treatment of Borderline Personality Disorder.* New York, NY: Guilford Press; 1993.
2. Linehan MM, Dimeff LA, Reynolds SK, et al. Dialectical behavior therapy versus comprehensive validation therapy plus 12-step for the treatment of opioid dependent women meeting criteria for borderline personality disorder. *Drug Alcohol Depend.* 2002;67(1):13–26.
3. Luoma JB, Kohlenberg BS, Hayes SC, Bunting K, Rye AK. Reducing self-stigma in substance abuse through acceptance and commitment therapy: model, manual development, and pilot outcomes. *Addict Res Theory.* 2008;16(2):149–165.

IV
Planning Treatment

45

Set the Stage
Spend One Visit Preparing to Make Significant Treatment Changes

Setting

Whether seeing a patient for the first time or seeing a well-established patient for another follow up visit, clinicians will at some point have to make a significant change in the treatment plan. One common scenario is decreasing the dose of a controlled substance which is no longer serving the patient, such as tapering a benzodiazepine or opioid prescription. A less contentious situation might be changing a patient's insulin regimen.

The Technique

Regardless of how welcome the change, major treatment changes should be preceded by adequate preparation and discussion with the patient. Spend a visit discussing the treatment plan and reviewing upcoming changes with the patient. Review with the patient why and how you think a change needs to be made. Solicit the patient's thoughts and feelings on the change and validate any concerns or fears. The time between the preparatory visit and the next visit, at which change is enacted, should be framed as an opportunity to consider possible challenges with the new treatment plan. The patient may be invited to contact you with any questions or concerns. When the patient returns, review your last discussion and any contact you have had with the patient in the interim prior to moving forward.

Sample Dialogue

Patient: I really need my benzodiazepines refilled.

Clinician: I know you have struggled with anxiety and have been prescribed benzodiazepines for a long time. I'm very concerned about the risks of taking these medications for so long.

> I know there are risks, we've talked about them, and I don't care. I just need a refill.

> I hear that you're concerned with getting a refill. We need to talk about a plan for your benzodiazepine use moving forward. That doesn't mean not refilling your prescription, but it does mean thinking about changes in the future. Are you willing to discuss this?

> As long as I can get a refill today, I'm willing to discuss it. I don't want to feel anxious, but I also don't want to feel so desperate when I'm running out.

> Let's talk about a plan that we can start at our next visit. I can refill your prescription today, then at our next visit we will start decreasing your dose.

Why This Works

Big changes in treatment need not be abrupt or unexpected. This technique allows the patient and clinician to spend more time—ideally an entire visit plus time between visits—setting the stage for significant changes in treatment. Patients (and clinicians!) can be afraid of change. Even when the current treatment plan is not achieving the shared goals of the patient and clinician, it is often easier to continue what is sort of working, or even what used to be working, rather than making drastic changes.

Especially when contentious, significant changes in treatment take time. Change is a multi-step process that proceeds through contemplation to preparation before, finally, enactment of change.[1] Contentious or unilateral treatment changes rush this process and generate conflict in the therapeutic relationship. By allowing time for examination and acceptance, this approach facilitates change happening more smoothly. The clinician has time to validate the patient's concerns, even if the patient does not ultimately agree with the plan. The clinician also feels less rushed, as an entire visit accommodates plentiful discussion of why the change is indicated and how it will happen. Though treatment changes sometimes need to be made unilaterally, validation and discussion maintains collaboration between the patient and clinician. Dedicating substantial time to the upcoming change reinforces its importance for both the patient and clinician. Thus, this technique enhances the patient-clinician relationship even when disagreement exists.

Clinicians sometimes need to proceed with treatment changes despite the patient's wishes. This limit-setting is difficult for most clinicians, but it is necessary for the patient's health. Fortunately, there is usually less conflict over these decisions than feared. For example, in the sample dialogue, the patient is initially reluctant to decrease their benzodiazepine regimen. Yet when the clinician sets a firm limit and invites further discussion, the patient actually reveals ambivalence around the medication and voices concerns about continuing the prescription. This patient now appears more contemplative about this medication than the clinician may have previously suspected.

Final Thoughts

A visit to set the stage for significant treatment changes allows exploration and validation of the patient's concerns. The clinician can better safeguard the therapeutic alliance
notwithstanding potential disagreement over the treatment plan. Sometimes, however,
there is insufficient time to set the stage. Even if an entire visit cannot be dedicated to
discussing treatment changes, dedicating at least a shorter portion of the visit to discussing change can still be helpful.

Reference

1. Prochaska JO, DiClemente CC, Norcross JC. In search of how people change. Applications to
   addictive behaviors. *Am Psychol.* 1992;47(9):1102–1114.

The authors would like to thank Dr. James Haug for his contributions to the development of this technique.

46

Fish for Change Talk
Guide the Patient Into Talking About Behavior Change More Quickly

ALEX KIPP, MD, MALS

Setting

Motivational interviewing (MI) techniques help clinicians put patients in the driver's seat to make healthy decisions and enact positive behavior change.[1] The clinician conducting MI typically helps the patient frame their reasons both for and against behavior change. But when the clinician focuses too much on motivations that sustain the patient's unhealthy behaviors, there is a risk of making change more difficult for the patient.

Technique

Instead of focusing on why the patient is doing the unhealthy behavior, ask more questions about what the patient can do to change that behavior. MI describes a patient's statements regarding their health behaviors as falling into one of two categories: "sustain talk," which are the reasons for the patient to continue their behavior, and "change talk," the reasons to change said behavior. Acknowledge a patient's sustain talk when it arises then quickly move on to explore the change talk thoroughly. Most of the conversation should be spent discussing and emphasizing change. The clinician may have to fish for these change statements—when change talk happens, the clinicians should re-emphasize it and ask follow-up questions. For example, instead of asking, "What do you like about smoking?" shift to, "What would you like about not smoking?" Focus on the successes of the future, not the failures of the past.

Sample Dialogue

Patient: I would really like to stop smoking, but I keep trying to quit and it never sticks!

Clinician: Most people find quitting smoking is really hard. What benefits would you notice if you stopped smoking?

Well, I would save a lot of money, and it would be easier to keep up with my kids.

Spending time with your kids is important.

Yeah, and I'm worried that if I don't stop smoking, I'm going to get cancer and die before they grow up.

So quitting smoking would get you feeling better now and it would help you stay healthy in the long run. Is that a fair summary?

Yeah, all those things, but I just don't know if I can stick with it! It's too frustrating to try and fail.

It's hard for lots of people to stay away from smoking after they've quit. Once you've quit, what sorts of things do you think you could do to handle those urges?

Well, I could chew gum, or go for a walk…

Why This Works

Most management and prevention of chronic disease rests on the patient's shoulders. Clinicians can prescribe medication, make expert recommendations, and provide as much support as necessary, but only the patient can make the decision to change. MI is a tremendous resource for helping clinicians cultivate patients' desire and ability to change. Clinicians who use an MI approach are far more successful in helping patients improve health-promoting behaviors.[2] Yet as influential and helpful as MI is, clinicians (particularly when running low on time) must be careful not to spend more time discussing why patients are sustaining negative behavior than discussing how patients can change. Patients typically understand how their behaviors negatively impact their health. Inadvertently over-emphasizing reasons why change is difficult may only solidify those thoughts, particularly when those thoughts go unchallenged by the clinician.

It is important to recognize and validate the patient's motivations for unhealthy behaviors, but then it is more important to elicit and highlight change talk. The patient's reasons for maintaining unhealthy behaviors are often obvious—for example, they enjoy how they feel when they smoke. In fishing for change talk, the clinician encourages the patient to visualize a future in which the patient demonstrates the health-promoting behavior; the patient is encouraged to imagine the benefits of the behavior and what life looks like after making that change.

In the sample dialogue, the clinician repeatedly validates the patient's reasons for change and transitions to strategies the patient envisions using to stop smoking. The longer and more often a patient imagines doing a health-promoting behavior, the more realistic that behavior begins to feel.[3] The patient does not need to commit to changing their behavior by the encounter's end for this technique to be successful. Even imagining behavior change for five minutes can plant seeds of change that will flower in the future. Consider writing down the patient's reasons for changing behavior as well as planned steps to changing that behavior. Building on a conversation from the last encounter saves time and energy for the clinician and fosters an ongoing, collaborative attitude during the visit. As the patient and clinician meet over multiple encounters, the clinician can build on the change talk with further exploration of the patient's reasons and ability to change their behavior.

Final Thoughts

In motivational interviewing, clinicians convey that they accept the patient as they are, and approach the encounter with compassion, collaboration, and curiosity. This is helpful to remember as the main pitfall of fishing for change talk is that the patient feels unheard when the clinician shifts too rapidly to focus on change talk. Validating the motivations underlying negative behaviors is important and helps the clinician build credibility with the patient which is necessary to later emphasize change talk. This technique can be difficult for patients who are resistant to change or who remain pre-contemplative regarding their behavior change. However, as the clinician gains skill in MI and develops a stronger therapeutic relationship, it is possible to elicit change talk out of even the most resistant patient!

References

1. Miller WR, Rollnick S. *Motivational Interviewing: Helping People Change*. 3rd edition. New York, NY: Guilford Press; 2002.
2. Hettema J, Steele J, Miller W. A meta-analysis of research on motivational interviewing treatment effectiveness (MARMITE). *Annu Rev Clin Psychol*. 2005;1:91–111.
3. Schwartz JM, Begley S. *The Mind and the Brain*. New York, NY: HarperCollins; 2002.

47

Imagine the Future
Envision the Patient's Healthy Life in Order to Prioritize Treatment Goals

Setting

Some patients present with several, co-morbid physical, psychiatric, and social complaints that leave the clinician uncertain how to prioritize. The patient may be unclear which issue is most important to them, or perhaps the urgency of conditions varies from one appointment to the next—one week the patient's back pain requires attention, the next week housing is the most significant concern. Both the patient and clinician begin to feel as though a lot is happening during visits yet there is a sense of little progress, frustration, and impatience.

The Technique

Ask, "If everything goes well, what does life look like for you 4 or 6 weeks from now?" Patients may respond, "I won't have any pain," but ask them to imagine the next step. Focus on behaviors rather than the presence of somatic or psychiatric symptoms. What would you be doing? How would you spend your day? What would you be enjoying? Some patients will share that life would be better if they had relationships, a different job, or something unrelated to the clinical visit. When the work being done in the visit feels unrelated to the patient's goals, discuss this discrepancy with the patient.

Sample Dialogue

Patient: I just don't know what I need. My back hurts, these headaches are really bothering me, my medications don't work well, my depression and anxiety are disabling. What am I supposed to do?

Clinician: You do have a lot going on, that's true. It's almost tough to know where to start. Let me ask, if everything went well for you, what would your life look like 4 weeks from now?

> Well, I wouldn't have pain.

> If you didn't have pain, what would your days look like? What would you do? Where would you spend your time?

> It would be nice to spend some time at the gym—or look for work. I could keep the house clean.

> Spending time at the gym, working, keeping the house clean. Those sound like healthy activities. Let's talk about what keeps you from doing those things.

Why This Works

Many patients have multiple psychiatric and medical conditions, and co-morbidity is increasingly frequent.[1,2] Typically these patients also describe social stressors related to relationships, employment, and housing. These presentations challenge clinicians' expertise, time management, and need to rely on outside consultation for treatment planning. Among these challenges is how to prioritize which condition requires immediate attention. Prioritization is even more difficult in cases where psychiatric morbidity complicates medical presentations like pain—in these instances, both conditions require attention simultaneously.

Constantly chasing a long list of individual problems is frustrating and unrewarding for the clinician and patient alike. This technique moves the clinical interview away from a laundry list of symptoms and towards goal setting and functioning. In cognitive behavior therapy, patients are taught to understand how their behaviors can improve how they feel and how they think about themselves and the world. Changing behaviors represents both a goal of treatment as well as a form of treatment itself. In the sample dialogue, the patient has a list of physical and emotional concerns. If this patient waits for all these issues—pain, anxiety, depression—to improve before trying to do the activities that give him joy, he is unlikely to feel better. It is difficult to feel good if you are not doing the things you enjoy! The clinician in this example did not let the patient get away with saying "less pain;" rather, the patient was pressed to behavioralize his answer.

This technique defines and prioritizes treatment goals in a way that a list of chief complaints cannot. Resolution of these problems is not necessarily required to achieve treatment goals. For instance, the patient may still experience some back pain and depression even as they enjoy going to the gym. Changing the topic of conversation to functional goals further allows the clinician to discuss the importance of behavior change to altering symptoms. In this example, the patient's physical activity is more likely to improve his somatic symptoms[3] and depression.[4] Whereas this technique works well with patients facing multiple concurrent co-morbidities and stressors, chapter 38 describes a similar technique that is better suited to the assessment and monitoring of more discrete syndromes (e.g., chronic pain).

Cognitive behavior therapy posits that thinking positively leads one to feel and act differently. In a simplistic example, we must first think of an activity (like exercise) before we do it. Similarly, the patient must know what successful treatment looks like before achieving it; imagining a better life is necessary to making that better life a reality. In the case of extreme co-morbidity, the clinician can use the patient's functional goals to prioritize particular concerns and identify the barriers to accomplishing these self-stated goals.

Final Thoughts

Many patients with high co-morbidity have histories of trauma, severe anxiety, or borderline personality disorder.[5] One symptom of these conditions is a propensity for the patient to feel invalidated and unheard. This technique works best when the clinician and patient agree on a general approach to treatment—for example, what the diagnosis is and how to balance medication and non-pharmacologic treatments—thereby allowing the clinician to challenge the patient to generate behavioral goals. In this dialogue, the clinician repeatedly validates the patient's statements through simple repetition before moving on to apply the technique. Once the goals of treatment have been re-stated in a way that emphasizes a functional goal, both the clinician and patient can spend less time discussing a litany of individual symptoms and more time pursuing the goals that represent a healthy, fulfilling life for the patient.

References

1. Kessler RC, Chiu WT, Demler O, Merikangas KR, Walters EE. Prevalence, severity, and comorbidity of 12-month DSM-IV disorders in the National Comorbidity Survey Replication. *Arch Gen Psychiatry*. 2005;62(6):617–627.
2. Ward BW, Schiller JS, Goodman RA. Multiple chronic conditions among US adults: a 2012 update. *Prev Chronic Dis*. 2014;11:E62.
3. Rantonen J, Karppinen J, Vehtari A, et al. Effectiveness of three interventions for secondary prevention of low back pain in the occupational health setting: a randomised controlled trial with a natural course control. *BMC Public Health*. 2018;18(1):598.
4. Sukhato K, Lotrakul M, Dellow A, Ittasakul P, Thakkinstian A, Anothaisintawee T. Efficacy of home-based non-pharmacological interventions for treating depression: a systematic review and network meta-analysis of randomised controlled trials. *BMJ Open*. 2017;7(7):e014499.
5. Dubovsky AN, Kiefer MM. Borderline personality disorder in the primary care setting. *Med Clin North Am*. 2014;98(5):1049–1064.

48

Prescribe Change

Use a Prescription Pad to Emphasize Non-Pharmacologic Interventions

Setting

Clinicians often provide treatment recommendations other than medication prescriptions. These recommendations may include tracking symptoms, considering potential treatment options, or other behavioral interventions like exercise. The result of these conversations is essentially a homework assignment to be reviewed at the next session, but often these recommendations feel less weighty and urgent than similar discussions of medication changes. The clinician and patient should mutually buy into the importance of non-pharmacologic interventions.

The Technique

Use a paper prescription sheet to "prescribe" psychotherapeutic assignments or behavioral change. The recommendation may be to write a list of pros and cons around behavioral change (as in Figure 48.1) or to track symptoms (as in chapter 31). The prescription should include clear instructions—for example, a format for tracking symptoms, a guide to weigh decisions, or the frequency and nature of behavioral instructions. The patient takes this prescribed instruction with them, and the clinician should document the assignment for reference at the next visit. It is vital for the clinician to follow-up on the assignment at the next encounter.

Sample Dialogue

Clinician: We've been talking about your weight for a long time now; it seems you are hesitant to make some changes in your lifestyle.

Patient: I think that's right. It's just really difficult to take even the first steps, especially since I generally feel good. I just don't feel like I need to lose weight right now.

It is difficult, and I have a proposal. Making these tough decisions requires some thought, and there are pros and cons to every decision. I suggest you think through these using a chart like this, and we can review it at our next visit. Then we'll see where you are with this decision.

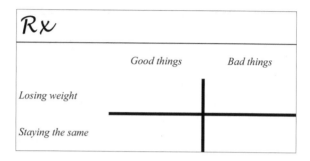

Figure 48.1

Why This Works

All clinical encounters involve work done by the clinician to heal the patient. This expected routine represents a ritual expected by patients, family, and clinicians alike.[1] The use of these rituals contributes to the healing power of allopathic and alternative forms of medicine.[2] One reason placebos are used in research is to isolate the active ingredients of medications from the accompanying healing rituals that come with those medications. Even the efficacy of at least one surgery has been disproven upon comparison to convincing sham procedures.[3]

Discussing and prescribing medications is fraught with ritual: the clinician brings esoteric expertise, provides access to medications not otherwise available to the patient, and then writes a particular dosing and frequency for the patient using terminology and abbreviations indecipherable to patients. When patients return, prescribers discuss adherence, side effects, and dose changes. These habits reinforce the idea of medications as vital to the patient's well-being and even as a third partner in the clinician-patient relationship dedicated to the patient's health.[4] Psychiatrists have similarly inculcated rituals when conducting psychotherapy such as how the therapy hour is organized, where the patient and therapist sit, and how payment is handled.

This technique allows the clinician to leverage the rituals of medication prescribing to briefer patient encounters involving decision-making and behavioral change. The prescription pad emphasizes the importance of the recommendation, and the clinician's belief in its importance. Just as the clinician "gifts" the patient a medication,[4] this technique allows the clinician to reinforce that behavioral treatments are evidence-based and scientific interventions being prescribed by a knowledgeable professional. Patients are accustomed to safeguarding the piece of paper on which a prescription is written,[5] and the clinician takes advantage of this habit to help patients appropriately value a non-pharmacologic intervention. In a world of electronic health records, the clinician may need to find a prescription pad typically reserved for computer downtime (or use the copy-proof paper from the prescription printer).

Final Thoughts

Many prescribers fall into the trap of over-emphasizing medication treatment because our patients do, too. We fail to give sufficient attention and thoughtfulness to behavioral change and difficult decisions. This shortcoming does the patient no service. While properly using medication is a life-saving intervention for many patients, many medical and psychiatric conditions are better treated with psychotherapies and behavioral changes. This technique reminds the clinician as well as the patient of the importance of non-pharmacologic treatments.

References

1. Welch JS. Ritual in western medicine and its role in placebo healing. *J Relig Health.* 2003;42(1):21–33.
2. Kaptchuk TJ. The placebo effect in alternative medicine: can the performance of a healing ritual have clinical significance? *Ann Intern Med.* 2002;136(11):817–825.
3. Moseley JB, O'Malley K, Petersen NJ, et al. A controlled trial of arthroscopic surgery for osteoarthritis of the knee. *N Engl J Med.* 2002;347(2):81–88.
4. Tutter A. Medication as object. *J Am Psychoanal Assoc.* 2006;54(3):781–804.
5. Christensen RC. 'Prescribing' behavioral and lifestyle changes. *Curr Psychiatry.* 2006;5(7):120.

49

Ask the Patient's Beliefs Regarding Medications

Understand What Patients Think Medications Will Do for Them to Clarify Treatment and Improve Adherence

Setting

Patients have many different beliefs about medications. Some interpret medications as a panacea or even permission to continue current problematic behaviors. For example, a patient who starts medication to lower their cholesterol may feel they do not need to modify their diet. Another patient with mild hypothyroidism might believe that a prescription will give them more energy, resolve their depression, and jumpstart efforts at weight loss. On the other hand, there are patients who go to great lengths to avoid medications. Sometimes this avoidance is motivating. Consider the patient with pre-diabetes who successfully loses weight through dietary changes in order to avoid diabetic medication. But often this avoidance is detrimental and increases the risk for later complications. Understanding patient beliefs about medications is helpful in improving adherence and engagement in treatment planning.

The Technique

After discussing the risks, benefits, and alternatives of recommended medications, solicit the patient's thoughts about taking the medication: "How do you feel about taking this medication?" Probe for specifics and explicitly ask if the patient will take the medication. Pay particular attention to comments the patient makes about potential fears, behavior changes, or the likelihood of adherence. If the patient suggests they will not be adherent, invite them to share with you their reasoning. Remain open and non-judgmental; the initial goal is obtaining information rather than providing feedback.

Sample Dialogue

Clinician: Since we've reviewed the specifics of the medication, I'm wondering how you feel about taking it?

Patient: It's fine, just send it to my pharmacy.

Are you going to try this medication?

> I don't know, maybe. We'll see.

You sound unsure. Can you help me understand what it is about the medication that makes you unsure?

> I don't know, I'm just not a person who takes medications. Like if I have to start taking a pill every day now, who knows how many medications I'll end up taking?

That is scary to think about it when you put it like that. Let's talk about how one medication might help you avoid having to take additional medications in the future.

Why This Works

As a clinician, you may frequently prescribe medications to patients. It is easy to fall into the habit of assuming the patient will simply follow recommendations, take the medication, and return in a few months with improved symptoms. And sometimes this happens! But when it does not, treatment failure can be frustrating and disappointing for both the patient and clinician. Treatment is more likely to be successful when expectations are realistic and barriers to adherence addressed early.

Patient's beliefs around medications play an important role in adherence; patients who describe adherence as a strong personal belief are more likely to take medications consistently.[1] This technique allows the clinician to pro-actively address expectations around medications that might ultimately interfere with the patient's treatment goals. For example, the patient's beliefs may lead them to continue unhealthy habits or harbor overly ambitious hopes for how the medications will be helpful. Acting on these expectations, patients may not achieve treatment goals (e.g., better cholesterol levels) and quickly grow discouraged. Some patients—like the one in the sample dialogue—have fears around what it means to take medications and are likely to discontinue the medication in the absence of a discussion to specifically address those concerns. Sometimes patient's concerns include modifiable risk factors for non-adherence, such as regimen complexity or concurrent depression.[2] The only way for the clinician to allay these concerns and align with the patient's goals is to discuss them.

Using this technique builds an understanding of the patient's perspective in a way that allows the clinician to dispel misconceptions and problem-solve barriers to adherence.[3] The process of exploring the patient's perspective not only allows specific barriers to adherence to be addressed but also strengthens the clinician-patient relationship. This process is itself therapeutic and vital to treatment: the quality of the clinician-patient relationship is associated with medication adherence.[4]

Final Thoughts

Patients have different beliefs about medications. These beliefs influence patient's adherence to medication and the success of the treatment plan. Some patients are not able or willing to discuss their beliefs about medications. In these instances, patients are unlikely to participate wholeheartedly in treatment. Better approaches might be to set the stage (chapter 45) for starting a medication later or to spend more time understanding the patient's treatment goals in order to better contextualize the benefits of a medication.

References

1. Massey EK, Tielen M, Laging M, et al. Discrepancies between beliefs and behavior: a prospective study into immunosuppressive medication adherence after kidney transplantation. *Transplantation*. 2015;99(2):375–380.
2. Ghimire S, Castelino RL, Lioufas NM, Peterson GM, Zaidi ST. Nonadherence to medication therapy in haemodialysis patients: a systematic review. *PLoS ONE*. 2015;4:10(12):e0144119.
3. Derksen F, Bensing J, Lagro-Janssen A. Effectiveness of empathy in general practice: a systematic review. *Br J Gen Pract*. 2013;64(606):e76–84.
4. van der Laan DM, Elders PJM, Boons CCLM, Beckeringh JJ, Nijpels G, Hugtenburg JG. Factors associated with antihypertensive medication non-adherence: a systematic review. *J Hum Hypertens*. 2017;31(11):687–694.

50
Anticipate Challenges
Be Specific in Planning Ahead and Removing Obstacles to Treatment Success

Setting

Patients are quick to agree to a treatment plan because they like the idea of improvement and are averse to consider the inherent challenges. Clinicians want to encourage the patient's optimism, but they often feel skeptical of the likelihood of success given their extensive experience with patients who are non-adherent with medications or behavioral interventions. To implement a treatment plan with high hopes and then fail is discouraging. The clinician must balance optimism and realism by understanding potential obstacles to treatment and equipping the patient to overcome them.

The Technique

In discussing the treatment plan, challenge the patient to voice obstacles to adherence. Examples of obstacles may come from the patient's past history of non-adherence or from the clinician's experiences with other similar patients. Having made these potential obstacles explicit, imagine solutions with the patient. The clinician can contribute ideas but should do so sparingly: solutions generated by the patient are more likely to be implemented.

Sample Dialogue

Patient: Yeah, this will probably work.

Clinician: You sound optimistic, but it's difficult to check your blood sugars so frequently. What do you mean by "probably"? What is going to be challenging about making this work?

Well, for example, I know my friend is having a party next month, and I don't want to check my sugars right in the middle of the party. It's so embarrassing!

I appreciate that. Have you run into a situation like this before?

Well, I check my sugars at work sometimes. It's awkward, but I've told a few friends at work about my situation so they cover for me.

That sounds like a great solution. Would something similar work at your friend's party?

Why This Works

Even the best treatment plans fail if not put in action. Oftentimes patients return to care frustrated at being unable to stick with behavioral changes or adhere to prescribed regimens. The risk of frustration should be mitigated through a realistic appraisal of how feasible the recommended treatment is. The best way to develop a realistic treatment plan is to have a specific sense of obstacles to success.

Generally, clinicians are not good at predicting patients' ability to enact change.[1] Patients themselves are not much better—patients' intentions do not mirror their eventual behavior.[2] Imagining what obstacles may separate intention from actual behavior requires creativity and prompting by the clinician. During the encounter, patients may overestimate their ability to enact change for fear of disappointing the clinician or out of over-optimism about the prospects for success. The clinician cannot presume that the patient will spontaneously envision barriers to treatment.

This technique helps identify specific barriers to treatment planning. In clinical medicine, past is often prologue. The patient's and clinician's personal experience are excellent sources of information about potential barriers—and solutions. In the sample dialogue, the patient shares a very specific concern about leaving a social situation to check their blood sugar after having just voiced unbridled optimism of success. Left unspoken, the patient would have been likely to remain silently anxious about this barrier to treatment. However, the clinician recognizes that this appears to be a problem that has been solved previously and helps the patient apply their prior success to the current predicament. The more specific a challenge to adherence can be described, the more effective proposed solutions will be.

Another success of the example encounter is that the solution came from the patient. There are several reasons that patient-generated solutions are more likely to be enacted and effective. Most simple is that patients have the best sense of their own challenges and therefore have the potential to create better solutions. The patient is also more likely to commit to and remember (or re-discover) a solution of their own than the clinician's. A more subtle reason involves the importance of the patient's sense of self-efficacy for enacting change. Patients' ability to translate intention into behavior reflects their perceptions of how difficult it is to change and their own efficacy to enact that change.[3] When the patient generates their own solution, their self-efficacy is reinforced, and the difficulty of the perceived problem is diminished.

Final Thoughts

For this technique to be most effective, patients must be willing to admit that treatment adherence may be difficult. Patients unwilling to admit such will also have a difficult time frankly describing challenges at later follow-up appointments. Under these circumstances, the clinician might consider normalizing how difficult it is to enact change and emphasize enhancing the patient's motivation for adherence. Eventually, the patient will bring their challenges to the encounter on their own schedule, not the clinician's.

References

1. Kelly MP, Barker M. Why is changing health-related behaviour so difficult? *Public Health.* 2016;136:109–116.
2. Faries MD. Why we don't "Just do it": understanding the intention-behavior gap in lifestyle medicine. *Am J Lifestyle Med.* 2016;10(5):322–329.
3. Ajzen I. The theory of planned behavior. *Organ Behav Hum Decis Process.* 1991;50(2):179–211.

51

Experiment With Change

Introduce Change as Something the Patient Can Simply Try Out— No Commitment Necessary!

Setting

Implementing behavioral change can be daunting for patients. Change is complicated by logistical barriers, ambivalence, uncertainty, and the force of habit. In the course of understanding the patient's motivation for change, clinicians sometimes struggle to help the patient move from contemplating and preparing to enacting the first steps of change. The patient may express hesitancy about or fear of being able to adhere to change. Failing at this stage frustrates clinicians who feel that change is so close, yet so far.

The Technique

Propose trying out the discussed behavioral change for a pilot period to see how it goes. "How about looking at these changes as an experiment we're going to try for the next few weeks until our follow-up appointment?" Emphasize that any changes are only a trial run, and ask about the patient's progress at the next encounter. This follow-up visit is an opportunity to review successes, failures, obstacles, and new solutions.

Sample Dialogue

Clinician: How do you feel about starting to take a walk every day?

Patient: I don't know, it seems like a lot. I don't think I'm going to be able to do that.

Going for a walk every day is a big change from what you're doing now. What do you think about considering the time until our next appointment as an experiment with doing things differently?

Like just giving the daily walk a try?

Exactly, just giving the daily walk a try. It will be helpful to see how it goes even just for a short time so that we can review what worked and what didn't at our next appointment.

Why This Works

Patients can feel fearful and overwhelmed when faced with the recommendation for a significant change in behavior.[1] They may be pessimistic about the prospects for success. This pessimism often stems from an "all or nothing" perspective, that changes must be made completely or else there is no point in changing at all. In this state of mind, patients over-emphasize obstacles and feel little incentive to attempt change in the (mis-)perceived face of certain failure.

This technique challenges these cognitive distortions.[2] Introducing change as an experiment conveys that attempting to change is still, indeed, change. New patterns of behavior may be short-lived or limited but are still commendable. The clinician lowers their own expectations from achieving lasting change to merely acquiring more data on how the patient feels and what is difficult about sustaining different behaviors. Both the clinician and patient are allowed permission to receive credit for success that is short of ideal. The stakes are lowered such that change feels like something that need merely be attempted—rather than maintained permanently. Lowering the perceived difficulty of enacting change and enhancing the patient's sense of self-efficacy improves the likelihood of successful behavioral change.[3]

Moreover, this technique introduces and normalizes the possibility of failure. Behavioral change does not proceed flawlessly, and success is never a foregone conclusion. Patients do not want to disappoint their clinicians or loved ones by making an open commitment to change that they cannot enact. Rather than fear failure, the patient should be encouraged to experience even small successes. And *any* success, no matter how small, should be celebrated and emphasized at follow-up visits. The clinician and patient should discuss what worked and what did not as a result of this experience, seek to minimize barriers, and replicate facilitating factors.

Final Thoughts

The ultimate goal of this technique is to effect some behavioral change, no matter how small or infrequent. These small changes provide data for the patient to better resolve ambivalence over behavioral change and for the clinician to provide practical support for the patient to realize their goals. Some patients with highly rigid and dichotomous thinking styles have difficulty accepting change as merely an experience. They may dismiss the value of making partial or piecemeal changes. In these instances, the clinician might consider setting the stage for an experiment with change by raising the concept ahead of time (chapter 45).

References

1. Ajzen I. The theory of planned behavior. *Organ Behav Hum Decis Process*. 1991;50(2):179–211.
2. Beck AT, Rush AJ, Shaw BF, Emery G. *Cognitive Therapy of Depression*. New York, NY: Guilford Press; 1979.
3. Orji R, Vassileva J, Mandryk R. Towards an effective health interventions design: an extension of the health belief model. *Online J Public Health Inform*. 2012;4(3):ojphi.v4i3.4321.

52

Operationalize Improvement

Be Specific With the Patient About What "Better" Means

Setting

Patients often express that they want to feel "better" without specific steps or benchmarks by which this will be determined. The term better is most often used as a placeholder for a nonspecific improved level of functioning to which the patient aspires but has not identified how to achieve. Patients may return regularly for appointments despite having made minimal progress in following treatment recommendations. Patients can have a "I'll know it when I see it" perspective which leaves clinicians frustrated and perhaps hopeless, wondering if the patient's better will ever be attained.

The Technique

Be specific with the patient to understand what they mean when they say better. Focus on how the patient will function differently when they are better. What exactly will they be able to do that they are not able to do now? What keeps them from doing these things now? Ask questions to fully grasp what the patient wants their life and health to be like and also the barriers that they perceive to reaching their goals.

Sample Dialogue

> Patient: I always take my meds, but I always feel depressed. Why is it so hard to feel better?

> Clinician: What would be different if you felt better?

> I don't know. I'd just feel better. Things would be easier.

> Are there things that you would like to be able to do when you're better that you're not able to do now?

Yeah, I want to go on walks with my grandkids; that'd be nice.

What keeps you from going on walks with your grandkids now?

My feet hurt all the time, and I can't keep up with them.

That's frustrating. I wonder what would help with the pain in your feet and your energy so you can go on walks with you grandkids.

Well, I guess it would help if I took my nerve pain medicine. And I know I have more energy when I sleep well so I should probably follow those sleep recommendations you gave me.

Why This Works

Vague goals are epitomized by the patient's use of the phrase "feel better." However, such vague goals quickly evolve into elusive ones. Why would a patient express their treatment goal vaguely? Perhaps the patient is genuinely uncertain as to what they want. More often it is easier for the patient to say they simply want to be better than to consider all of the challenges to better health—and even new challenges they may face when they are actually better. In these cases, the clinician needs to operationalize what the patient means by better. What would the patient *do* differently? What does living a healthy life look like? Goals should be specific, quantifiable, and realistic.[1]

Operationalizing better helps the patient and clinician develop, share, and advance treatment goals. The clinician gains an understanding of the patient's current situation and barriers to improvement.[2] The patient is able to envision successful treatment and anticipate the necessary steps towards improvement.[3] This technique is especially helpful for patients who return routinely for appointments but appear to have had no progress towards adherence or treatment. Often these patients feel so overwhelmed with perceived obstacles to improving their health that they opt to do nothing or very little. Empathetically working with patients to identify their goals empowers them to make small but impactful changes.

In the sample dialogue, the patient initially has difficulty elaborating on the goals of treatment. A brief follow-up reveals one concrete goal—being able to take walks with their family. This goal is readily observed and could even be quantified via a tracking log. The clinician is then able to re-direct the interview from addressing a vague goal of feeling better to targeting specific barriers that stand in the way of explicit goals. This conversation feels more productive for both the patient and clinician. Other approaches for developing treatment goals are described in chapters 38 and 47.

Final Thoughts

Patients with vague goals frustrate clinicians. Achievable goals require clarity, and the clinician must connect specific goals to the treatment plan in order to enhance adherence. One pitfall of this technique is the potential for the patient to feel bombarded by questions from the clinician who is seeking to develop a behavioral target. Balance asking questions with validating statements to sustain the patient's energy and engagement in thought-provoking goal setting.

References

1. Doran GT. There's a S.M.A.R.T. way to write management's goals and objectives. *Mage Rev.* 1981;70(11):35–36.
2. Bratzke LC, Muehrer RJ, Kehl KA, Lee KS, Ward EC, Kwekkeboom KL. Self-management priority setting and decision-making in adults with multimorbidity: a narrative review of the literature. *Int J Nurs Stud.* 2015;52(3):744–755.
3. Coulter A, Entwistle VA, Eccles A, Ryan S, Shepperd S, Perera R. Personalized care planning for adults with chronic or long-term health conditions. *Cochrane Database Syst Rev.* 2015;(3):CD010523.

53

Frame Limit-Setting From the Patient's Perspective

Consider How Setting Effective Limits Will Improve the Patient's Care

DAVID KROLL, MD

Setting

Patients sometimes behave in ways that frustrate clinicians or disrupt the clinical environment. Such behaviors might be blatantly inappropriate (e.g., using insulting or abusive language) or reflect a poor understanding of how the healthcare system works (e.g., expecting the clinician to be available in the middle of the night). Caring for patients can be more difficult when they do not attend to social norms or clinical boundaries. Rather than simply complaining about patients' behaviors, clinicians should be prepared to productively call attention to the ways in which disruptive behaviors interfere with treatment.

The Technique

Clinical boundaries are limits set on expected behaviors in the treatment relationship. Clarify with the patient exactly how they are violating the clinical boundary. Then consider how erasing that boundary could negatively impact the patient's care, as opposed to how it bothers you or goes against a policy. If a patient has unrealistic expectations—for example, wants to call you at all hours of the day and night—there is a high likelihood that eventually you will fail to be available at the right time. In the case of an emergency, the patient's safety could even be compromised. Or if a patient behaves inappropriately in your office and you are distracted, you'll be more likely to make a mistake. Use the patient's perspective to frame feedback about problematic behaviors.

Sample Dialogue

Patient: Sorry to call you so late, but I can't remember when my next appointment is.

Clinician: I don't remember, either. If you call the office tomorrow when they're open, the staff will be able to tell you.

> Can't you look it up for me now? I might need to reschedule.

> I'm not near a computer right now. But even if I were, I can't reschedule the appointment. Only the office staff can do that. You'll get it done more quickly and reliably if you call them directly.

> I guess I'll call them tomorrow, then.

> Thank you. Going forward, please only page me for emergencies. If you page me for other reasons, I won't always know that your page is an emergency, and I'm more likely to miss something important.

Why This Works

Clinical boundaries exist not only to protect the clinician's feelings and time but also to guide patients in safely and efficiently accessing what they need. A patient's behavior may come across as disruptive even when their intentions are benign, but this behavior can still undermine treatment.[1] It is the clinician's professional responsibility to help patients optimize their likelihood of achieving the best possible outcomes.

So-called treatment-interfering behavior does, in fact, interfere with treatment. Some patients develop expectations based on idealization of their clinicians but thereby inevitably await disappointment.[2] Moreover, clinicians' negative feelings induced by problematic patient behaviors erode the doctor-patient relationship.[1] In extreme cases, resentful clinicians might even be provoked to punitive actions that do not have a clinical benefit[2] or unconsciously provide a lower quality of care as a consequence of burnout.[3] Upset and frustrated clinicians may find themselves setting limits for convenience rather than therapeutic effect.

Purposefully considering the limit from the patient's perspective ensures that the clinician's approach is aligned with the patient's needs—not simply the clinician's needs. Most patients do not naturally appreciate how limit-setting serves their interests.[2] Framing limit-setting in this way reduces the risk that a clinician's efforts to address problematic behaviors will be perceived as criticism, which can have a negative impact on the patient and will not change behavior.[4] In the sample dialogue, the clinician begins by explaining how calling the right person (in this case, the scheduling desk) is a more efficient way to obtain the desired goal (scheduling an appointment) than calling the clinician directly. When the patient pushes back, the clinician expands this feedback to point out how the boundary-crossing behavior (calling at an inappropriate time with a non-emergent request) makes it difficult to provide good care. This framework not only helps guide you when you are unsure of how to communicate the limit but also helps you decide whether to set the limit at all. When you are truly acting in the best interests of the patient, you know you are doing the right thing even if it feels uncomfortable in that moment.

Patients and clinicians do not always have the exact same goals for a clinical encounter, but there should be enough overlap between the clinician's and patient's goals for care to move forward.[5] Boundaries and limits should reflect the goals that the patient and clinician share—or don't share. This technique works because it incorporates the patient's goals for treatment as well as the clinician's limitations. Convincing anyone to follow advice is a much easier task when it means achieving a goal that is important to them.

Final Thoughts

The clinician will more likely succeed in setting therapeutic limits if those limits are communicated in a way that emphasizes their benefit to the patient. Patients are not easily fooled, and this technique only works when the limits you set honestly help you provide better care. If your attempt to set the limit provokes resistance, listen to what the patient says. It may uncover a problem on your end which you should be prepared to accept and fix.

References

1. Boland R. The "problem patient": modest advice for frustrated clinicians. *R I Med J (2013)*. 2014;97(6):29–32.
2. Groves JE. Taking care of the hateful patient. *N Engl J Med*. 1978;298(16):883–887.
3. Lu DW, Desden S, McCloskey C, Branzetti J, Gisondi MA. Impact of burnout on self-reported patient care among emergency physicians. *West J Emerg Med*. 2015;16(7):996–1001.
4. Hooley JM, Siegle G, Gruber SA. Affective and neural reactivity to criticism in individuals high and low on perceived criticism. *PLoS ONE*. 2012;7(9):e44412.
5. Sacheli LM, Aglioti SM, Candidi M. Social cues to joint actions: the role of shared goals. *Front Psychol*. 2016;6:1034.

54
Share Difficult Decisions
Give the Patient Options When Collaborating on a Treatment Plan With Which the Patient Is Reluctant to Engage

Setting

Clinicians sometimes need to make unilateral treatment decisions with which the patient does not agree and does not wish to comply. One example of this is tapering controlled substances such as opioids or benzodiazepines. Patients can be fearful when these conversations are brought up, and fear is often followed by anger, outrage, and threats to the clinician (such as leaving a bad review online) or to the patient (such as self-harm). In giving the patient the opportunity to choose among options as the treatment plan is created, patients are able to maintain a sense of self-efficacy and participation and see the treatment plan for what it is: a collaboration between clinician and patient with the patient's best interest in mind.[1]

The Technique

Give the patient several options for reaching the end goal in mind. For example, if you would like to stop your patient's benzodiazepine, offer them a choice in the tapering schedule. You might cut the original dose in half up front, then taper more slowly; or you might offer an alternative, more consistent taper. Both options result in discontinuing the medication in the same amount of time. The reason for the decrease and ideal timeline should be kept in mind, but usually there is some flexibility in crafting the treatment plan regardless of urgency. Offer the patient at least two but no more than four different treatment options and emphasize that the patient will choose how you proceed. Clearly communicate that "none of the above" is not a valid option.

Sample Dialogue

Clinician: We need to talk about our treatment plan. I'm concerned about your chronic prescription for benzodiazepines as there are many risks associated with use.

Patient: I can't stop; it's the only thing that helps.

> I can agree this medication has been helpful for you in the past, but it's not something that is safe to continue. That said, we have options in how we proceed. Can we talk about the options?

> I don't know. I've tried everything and nothing has worked for me.

> I hear what you're saying. Let's look at how we can make the transition work for you. One option is to eliminate one of the four doses you take every day. I know you've mentioned that sometimes you don't take the noon dose so maybe it would be easiest to eliminate that dose. Or, we could reduce all four doses a little bit. But it's up to you to choose how we go about this. What do you think?

> Well, since I have to choose, I would like to decrease all those doses a little, so I still have some medication to take throughout the day.

Why This Works

Rarely do people enjoy being told what to do and even more rarely when the directive is authoritarian. Shared decision-making is a more effective way of working with patients.[2] This technique applies concepts from shared decision-making in a situation where the clinician is setting limits on treatment.

In the sample dialogue, the clinician is firm in explaining the available options for decreasing a medication dose. The boundaries of the available options are set early—this medication needs to be discontinued, but within those parameters there are multiple ways to achieve this goal. When the patient is given options within these limits, they better engage in the decision-making process. The end goal of discontinuing a medication is implicitly accepted as inevitable, and the patient's investment in the process generates acceptance of the ultimate decision. Although the overall goal of medication discontinuation may be undesirable, the patient's preferences are reflected in the treatment plan.[3] This technique works best when the upcoming decision is anticipated in preceding encounters. Groundwork helps the patient accept the upcoming change and makes clear the clinician's commitment both to enforcing some end goal (e.g., medication discontinuation) and also to incorporating the patient's preferences (e.g., the taper schedule). Discussing the change over at least two appointments is ideal.

Limit-setting is a difficult but necessary part of clinical practice. Clinicians want to help patients feel better, but it is unsound to acquiesce to patient preferences when those preferences result in harm to the patient. An unfortunate example of this is the practice of opioid overprescribing for pain that has become a major contributor to the current opioid epidemic.[4] Clinicians have a responsibility to keep patients safe including setting limits when necessary. In situations when there is disagreement over the treatment plan, the clinician's approach may not be to move the limit so much as understand and validate the patient's concerns through a collaborative treatment plan.

Final Thoughts

The need for a unilateral change in treatment might be easy to identify, but these changes are difficult to execute. One reason they are hard to execute is clinicians' discomfort with setting limits. This technique is useful for generating patient acceptance of the undesired treatment decision. In so doing, this technique also helps the clinician feel comfortable that they are incorporating the patient's preferences in treatment. A collaborative relationship requires give-and-take by both the patient and clinician; neither person can dictate treatment.

References

1. Barry MJ, Edgman-Levitan S. Shared decision making: the pinnacle of patient-centered care. *N Engl J Med.* 2012;366(9):780–781.
2. Charles C, Gafni A, Whelan T. Shared decision-making in the medical encounter: what does it mean? (or it takes at least two to tango). *Soc Sci Med.* 1997;44(5):681–692.
3. Elwyn G, Frosch D, Thomson R, et al. Shared decision making: a model for clinical practice. *J Gen Intern Med.* 2012;27(10):1361–1367.
4. Markary MA. Overprescribing is a major contributor to opioid crisis. *BMJ.* 2017;359:j492.

55

Define Efficacy for Medication Changes

Understand the Patient's Goals and How They Will Know If a Medication Change Is Working

Setting

Patients sometimes request changes to medication regimens, or that new medications be prescribed, when they feel a current regimen is not working. Perhaps the patient feels a new medicine or higher dosage will be more effective. Or, they may feel strongly about starting a medication that is heavily advertised. Sometimes patients' beliefs about medications are accurate and sometimes not. When considering a medication change, whether at the request of the patient or otherwise, it helps to define together how you will determine if the change is working—before making the change.

The Technique

Ask the patient, "How will we know if the medication change is working?" Be specific and focus on objectives that can be reported in a yes or no manner. Behavioral or quantifiable objectives are most helpful. For example, if the medication change is to address pain, the objective might be participating in physical therapy or going for a walk daily. Or, for anxiety medication, the objective might be going to the store at a busy time or attending a social function. Some changes might involve objective measures such as a lower blood pressure. Collaborate with the patient on the definition of "working" and assess progress towards that goal at your next appointment.

Sample Dialogue

Patient: I really need more pain medicine; what I'm taking now just isn't working.

Clinician: Let's talk about making adjustments. How would we know if any medication change we make is working?

I wouldn't be in pain.

Alright, your pain would improve. What would you be doing after the pain improves that you are not doing now?

Well, I want to be able to take my dog on a walk every day. I can't do that right now because of the pain.

That's a great goal. Let's get specific: How often will you be walking, and how far?

Well, he needs to go out a few times a day though not that far. I'd like to be able to take him out three times each day and go two blocks.

Why This Works

An effective treatment relationship requires shared goals between the patient and clinician.[1] This technique makes those goals explicit. Even if the clinician has clear goals for the patient's health, the patient may have different priorities. Collaborating on and clarifying those priorities is helpful for both to feel treatment is worthwhile.[2]

A shared understanding of what constitutes medication efficacy is especially important for medication changes that are driven by subjectively reported symptoms (e.g., pain or anxiety). Working on subjectively reported symptoms is fine but should also be accompanied by measurable, behavioral goals. In the sample dialogue, the patient initially posited that an improvement in pain should be the goal for the medication change. The clinician acknowledged this concern, and then encouraged the patient to have a more concrete behavioral goal.

In defining objective goals for a medication change, the clinician and patient are more likely to agree on efficacy or, conversely, lack of efficacy. Agreed upon goals make it easier to reverse course on ineffective treatments. Inability to obtain a goal—for example, going for regular walks as proposed in the sample dialogue—can be helpful in explaining to the patient why a return to the previous medication regimen is indicated. This follow-up conversation can then focus on the patient's continued progress rather than defensiveness or disappointment over the failure of treatment. Setting a goal up front also helps the clinician who may be only reluctantly considering a prescription for, or increased dose of, a controlled substance: a clear rationale for any increase in medication dosing may later constitute the clear rationale for a decrease.

Final Thoughts

Clinicians and patients should establish a shared understanding of what constitutes efficacy for proposed medication changes. In an era when polypharmacy is common, this technique reduces the risks from ever larger medication regimens prescribed in service of uncertain targets. Goals should be clearly defined and agreed upon. One pitfall of this technique is seen with the patient who consistently comes to appointments requesting medication changes. Patients who perpetually focus on medication options at the exclusion of other treatments risk missing out on the benefits of non-pharmacologic treatments like physical therapy or psychotherapy. Often these patients struggle to realize their goals, and a re-consideration of behavioral changes is likely warranted (perhaps using the techniques in chapters 40 or 48).

References

1. Barry MJ, Edgman-Levitan S. Shared decision making: the pinnacle of patient-centered care. *N Engl J Med*. 2012;366(9):780–781.
2. Stanek S. Goals of care: a concept clarification. *J Adv Nurs*. 2017;73(6):1302–1314.

56

Help Patients Resist Urges
Review How Patients Can Refrain From Acting on Unhelpful Impulses

Setting

Urges to engage in unhelpful or harmful behaviors are experienced by everyone. These impulses range from mild annoyances, such as putting off an unfavorable chore, to potentially harmful behaviors, such as substance use. Fortunately, all urges will pass. Yet patients experiencing intense anxiety, mood symptoms, or cravings have difficulty adopting this perspective. The clinician can guide the patient to identify and handle urges.

The Technique

Helps patients recognize how urges always precede thoughts and behaviors. Be specific with the patient about what they are yearning to do—for example, smoke a cigarette or eat something unhealthy. Urges cannot be resisted if not first noticed. Discuss how the urge will pass on its own even if the patient does nothing. Solicit an example of when this happened. Different urges take different amounts of time to pass, but the urge will pass. As waiting for the urge to pass can be quite challenging, review with the patient how they can use behavioral coping skills to ride out the urge, for example, by using a mindfulness exercise or progressive muscle relaxation (chapter 11). Write a plan with the patient for how they will handle urges the next time they arise.

Sample Dialogue

> Patient: I always want something sweet after dinner. I know it isn't good for me, and I'm really trying to follow my diet.

> Clinician: Do you struggle with having dessert most nights?

> All the time! Sometimes even in the middle of the day. I just want something sweet. I feel powerless, like there's nothing I can do.

That urge to eat something you know you shouldn't is something that bothers a lot of people. The good news is that these urges always pass. Even if they might return later, they always pass in the moment. I imagine there are some times when you don't eat sweets, too.

I guess. I mean, I don't have dessert every single time I want it, so I know that the wanting feeling goes away.

Let's talk about how you might cope when that urge arises.

Why This Works

Everyone does things that are not in their best interest despite their best intentions. Engaging in undesired behaviors begins with the thought and urge to act. Giving into such urges often brings temporary feelings of pleasure—even if they later induce disappointment, guilt, shame, or hopelessness. Patients often feel urges are impossible to resist and that they have no option but to act on the urge when it is present. Or they feel they have to "white knuckle" through the urge when it arises, which is exhausting and not sustainable. Patients who have difficulty resisting urges are sometimes so convinced that avoiding action is impossible that their clinicians believe likewise. However, the feeling that a behavior is inevitable does not make it so.

Tolerating these urges is not comfortable, and we all have different abilities to tolerate distress. Distress tolerance arises from one's genetics, temperament, upbringing, and role models.[1] Despite the various contributors, distress tolerance is considered a long-standing trait even as it may vary over time in response to stress and illness.[2] Poor distress tolerance appears to be a risk factor for and closely associated with chronic anxiety, mood, pain, and addiction disorders.[3] Conversely, interventions to enhance coping skills that can be used when the patient is distressed may improve treatment of these conditions.[4] One such intervention, "urge surfing," has been described by mindfulness therapists.[5] Urge surfing employs mindfulness practices to help the patient get through the urge to act on a harmful behavior without acting on that behavior. Urge surfing is a potential useful tool for the patient and clinician as they review skills that can be helpful to the patient in resisting unwanted urges.

When the clinician reviews the patient's history, the patient often is able to describe episodes when an urge passed even without any efforts on the patient's part.[6] This reveals counterfactual evidence to the patient's protestations that urges are impossible to overcome: after all, the urge must have passed otherwise the patient would have acted on it. That the patient provides this evidence makes it more powerful and convincing. Upon the patient and clinician's mutual recognition that a particular action is not inevitable, the conversation may then cover specific coping skills. These identified skills may be codified into a crisis plan (chapter 58). Reinforcing the patient's ability to resist urges develops greater distress tolerance and greater capacity for positive change.

Final Thoughts

For patients and clinicians who feel change is impossible, this technique reminds us that not only is success possible, it has likely already been achieved in the past. But for this technique to be of use, patients must recognize urges as harmful. Patients who are ambivalent about their choices are unlikely to be willing to tolerate the distress associated with riding out urges. Such patients benefit from efforts to enhance their motivation for behavioral change, including the clinician's validating positive choices and helping the patient recognize those choices as aligned with their goals. In order to tolerate the distress of their urges, patients must understand why they are doing it.

References

1. Leyro TM, Zvolensky MJ, Bernstein A. Distress tolerance and psychopathological symptoms and disorders: a review of the empirical literature among adults. *Psychol Bull*. 2011;136(4):576–600.
2. Cummings JR, Bornovalova MA, Ojanen T, Hunt E, MacPherson L, Lejuez C. Time doesn't change everything: the longitudinal course of distress tolerance and its relationship with externalizing and internalizing symptoms during early adolescence. *J Abnorm Child Psychol*. 2013;41(5):735–748.
3. Brown RA, Lejuez CW, Kahler CW, Strong DR, Zvolensky MJ. Distress tolerance and early smoking lapse. *Clin Psychol Rev*. 2005;15(6):713–733.
4. Park CL, Russell BS, Fendrich M. Mind-body approaches to prevention and intervention for alcohol and other drug use/abuse in young adults. *Medicines (Basel)*. 2018;5(3):E64.
5. Bowen S, Marlatt A. Surfing the urge: brief mindfulness-based intervention for college smokers. *Psychol Addict Behav*. 2009;23(40):666–671.
6. Harris, R. The Happiness Trap. Boston, MA: Trumpeter Books; 2008.

57

Accept Ambivalence: "It's Okay Not to Change"

Allow Patients to Acknowledge and Accept When They Are Not Ready to Change

JODI ZIK, MD, AND MELANIE RYLANDER, MD

Setting

Patients often experience distress stemming from differences between the life they envision for themselves and the life they are living. In some cases, their behaviors might appear contrary to their stated goals—especially in the case of self-destructive behaviors like substance use or intentional self-harm. Patients might also lack the motivation or belief that they can change. In these situations, clinicians want to help the patient gain insight and facilitate self-efficacy. There are even a variety of techniques geared toward raising awareness of discrepancies between stated values and actions.[1] Yet, inevitably, some patients are not ready for change. In these instances, it is helpful to acknowledge this ambivalence in a manner that facilitates self-understanding as opposed to reinforcing a sense of failure.

The Technique

Instead of applying ever-increasing pressure to change the patient's behavior, use a short phrase, "It's okay not to change," to create an opening for discussion of the ambivalence around change. Clinicians can then use the patient's ambivalence as an opportunity to understand the reasons they are choosing not to change.

Sample Dialogue

Patient: I just can't bring myself to leave him.

Clinician: You've talked about how leaving him is a difficult decision for you. And I see how you really struggle over this.

Struggle is the word. I know this relationship is not good for me, but I can't bring myself to do anything about it. Why do I make such bad decisions all the time?

It's okay not to change. There are some good things about the way things are now.

Sure, like I don't have to worry about being alone.

That's a really normal fear. I'm wondering if we can talk more about that.

Why This Works

The decision to change can come in the future. In the present, acknowledging that someone is not ready to change is an opportunity to better understand the patient and how their actions minimize psychic distress.[2] Inherent to the patient's ambivalence are their perceptions regarding positive aspects of even dangerous behaviors, negative consequences of change, and fears associated with change. Many patients feel pressured by family, friends, and their clinicians to make some positive change. When patients do not or cannot change, they experience guilt. Removing the guilt and pressure to change creates space for the patient to share more about their motivating fears, anxieties, and desires.[2]

Many clinicians learn motivational interviewing to encourage healthy behavior change. However, many patients still elect not to change. Though clinicians might feel the need to change is obvious, we must recall the long provenance of our patients' choices. Early relationships and care environments serve as a scaffolding for how we will respond to and navigate our future world. Even dangerous behaviors have frequently developed as a coping skill to navigate previously experienced environments. Unfortunately, coping skills that were once helpful for hostile environments can become counterproductive once that environment changes. Labeling a patient as resistant and continuing to focus on the need for change—as opposed to helping them understand why they are not ready for change—leads to alienation and perpetuates feelings of failure and emotional invalidation. That is, the very same feelings that first laid the scaffolding for the maladaptive behaviors.

Clinicians grow frustrated with patients who engage in counterproductive behaviors that undermine their stated treatment goals. In this dialogue, the clinician probably agrees that the patient's relationship is not healthy. But we often do not understand our patients as well as we think. This technique helps us challenge our own assumptions about the patient's stated goals.[2] Reminding ourselves that not changing is a valid choice frees us to reflect with the patient on the decision ahead. It also reduces the pressure that clinicians feel to be responsible for the patient's choices. To be more committed to change than an ambivalent patient perpetuates our own frustration, clouds our empathy, and impedes our ability to help.

The decision to not change need not be a permanent one. Indeed, the resolution of ambivalence is fundamental to change.[3] Patients who are not ready for change will benefit from a better understanding of their own motivations underlying their current behaviors. Making patients feel judged or as if they have failed only alienates them from self-discovery and inculcates resistance to different choices.

Final Thoughts

Be careful that this technique does not outlive its expiration date. It is important to make an agreement with the patient that a decision to avoid change forever is not the goal. Rather, a decision not to change *yet* invites exploration of the behavior in the service of a treatment plan. Over time, the clinician will learn how to support their patient as the patient experiments with change, tolerating the loss of old comfortable habits while developing new, healthier patterns. This technique works well for many patients with personality disorders, depression, and/or anxiety as well as substance use. In these conditions, chronic, maladaptive patterns of behavior are strongly engrained.

References

1. Arkowitz H, Westra H. Introduction to the special series on motivational interviewing and psychotherapy. *J Clin Psychol*. 2009;65(11):1149–1155.
2. Engle D, Holiman M. A gestalt experiential perspective on resistance. *J Clin Psychol*. 2002;58(2):175–183.
3. Faris A, Cavell T, Fishburne J, Britton P. Examining motivational interviewing from a client agency perspective. *J Clin Psychol*. 2009;65(9):955–970.

58

Plan for a Crisis

Write a Three-Step Crisis Plan to Anticipate Patients' Triggers and Coping Skills

Setting

Many clinicians outside mental health settings worry about working with patients who have suicidal ideation, violent ideation, or substance use disorders. Their concerns partly involve a lack of familiarity with treatments for these conditions and a fear of the risks associated with these conditions, such as suicide. At a time when most Americans receive mental health treatment in non-specialty settings,[1] clinicians in all practice settings must be able to offer evidence-based interventions for these conditions. Crisis planning is a valuable psychotherapeutic intervention relevant to any clinical setting.

The Technique

Prepare a three-step crisis plan with the patient that identifies triggers, coping skills, and supportive contacts related to thoughts of suicide, violence, or substance use. The first step includes triggers that might make the patient feel worse or "red flags" that are associated with those feelings. Common triggers might include being alone at night when suicidal thoughts are worse or spending time with friends who encourage unhealthy drinking. In response to these triggers, the patient identifies things that they can do by themselves to improve their symptoms—perhaps engage in an enjoyable activity or walk away from a high-risk situation. In the third step, the patient identifies supportive persons who can help. Patients who struggle to identify supportive contacts might include the National Suicide Prevention Lifeline (in the US, 800-273-8255). Figure 58.1 illustrates a sample plan from the dialogue. The crisis plan should always be written down and a copy shared with the patient. Writing the plan briefly on an index card makes it easy to carry; there are electronic versions available for mobile devices, too.

Sample Dialogue

> Clinician: You've always said that the holidays are a difficult time to stay sober. Perhaps we should spend a few moments to prepare a crisis plan and anticipate how you are going to handle any cravings. What are some triggers that make your cravings to drink worse?

> Patient: Definitely holiday parties are difficult. Going shopping, too, I just always remember going to the mall and stopping for some food and drink—stores make me think of drinking.

> Holiday parties and going shopping are triggers for you, let me write that down. When you go to a party, say, how can you manage those cravings?

> Remind myself of my kids, they're why I got sober in the first place.

> That's great, maybe even take a look at their picture on your phone.

> Sure. I also just like to remind myself of my mantra, "One day at a time;" it's a nice reminder that these cravings will pass.

> Those are good skills. I know they've helped you before. Are there people you can call?

> I definitely call my partner first. My sponsor is usually around, too.

Crisis Plan

Triggers
1. Holiday parties
2. Shopping and being at the mall

Things I can do
1. Remind myself of my kids
2. Look at a picture of my kids
3. "One day at a time"

People to call
1. My partner
2. Support group sponsor

Figure 58.1

Why This Works

This crisis plan format was developed to help patients manage suicidal thoughts.[2] For patients with suicidal thoughts, brief safety planning improves the severity of suicidality, averts hospitalization, and reduces suicide attempts for months after the index encounter.[3-5] Safety planning is one of the best-supported and best-researched interventions for reducing self-harm. Why is this brief therapy so effective? First, it can be completed quickly when the patient is in crisis and receptive to teaching. Its simplicity makes the format easily understood by both clinicians and patients—there is little need for introduction or explanation. And it empowers patients by reminding them that they always have a choice available to them besides suicide. Finally, the inclusion of a supportive person is a pro-active strategy that encourages socialization. Distressed patients often erringly assume that they are alone and a burden to others even when family and friends may be readily, even eagerly, available to help them. A suicide safety plan should also include a reminder to restrict access to lethal means such as firearms and excess medications.

The three-step plan is adaptable to any number of psychiatric symptoms and helpful for all these same reasons. The clinician can help the patient recognize triggers that make relapse on drugs or alcohol more likely. Patients might describe precipitants of worsening anxiety, panic, or psychotic symptoms like hallucinations. In some instances, the term "trigger" feels less apropos than "red flag." Red flags are thoughts, feelings, or behaviors that the patient notices about themselves that are associated with worsening symptoms, for example, "I noticed that I start withdrawing from others," is a commonly reported red flag.

The clinician may assess the patient's ability to crisis plan to gauge how ably the patient will handle imminent stressors. The clinician sees the patient's coping style manifest through writing the crisis plan and can assist the patient in brainstorming coping skills or problem-solving. The clinician in the sample dialogue helped the patient operationalize the idea of using the patient's children as a coping skill by suggesting the use of a photograph. Coping skills should be realistic, safe, healthy, and not require participation by other persons. Many patients quickly offer, "Call somebody," as a coping skill; this should be reserved for step three.

Even when a crisis plan does not work perfectly, there are helpful lessons in reviewing the plan when the patient returns to care. (Ideally, a crisis plan should be saved in the patient's chart so that it can be reviewed and amended over time.) Questions to ask the patient in order to refine the crisis plan: Were the triggers or red flags correctly identified? Which coping skills did the patient try, and did they work? What coping skills should be added? What made it difficult to use the crisis plan?

Final Thoughts

Crisis planning is a quick, easy, and vital tool for managing a range of behavioral health symptoms. But a crisis plan is no substitute for a thorough assessment and treatment plan. It is merely a helpful adjunct that enhances treatment and aids in evaluation. Like all psychotherapies, crisis planning requires work on the patient's part. It is difficult to use a crisis plan for the first time in the midst of crisis. Their effectiveness is better with practice. Patients should be encouraged to review the plan daily—perhaps with a friend or family member—so that they are prepared to apply it when in distress. Most patients appreciate a simple sports metaphor to drive this point home: no team hits the field and expects to win without having practiced!

References

1. Wang PS, Lane M, Olfson M, Pincus HA, Wells KB, Kessler RC. Twelve-month use of mental health services in the United States: results from the National Comorbidity Survey replication. *Arch Gen Psychiatry.* 2005;62(6):629–640.
2. Stanley B, Brown GK. Safety planning intervention: a brief intervention to mitigate suicide risk. *Cognitive and Behavioral Practice.* 2012;19(2):256–264.
3. Miller IW, Camargo CA, Jr., Arias SA, et al. Suicide prevention in an emergency department population: the ED-SAFE study. *JAMA psychiatry.* 2017;74(6):563–570.
4. Stanley B, Brown GK, Currier GW, Lyons C, Chesin M, Knox KL. Brief intervention and follow-up for suicidal patients with repeat emergency department visits enhances treatment engagement. *Am J Public Health.* 2015:105(8):1570–1572.
5. Bryan CJ, Mintz J, Clemans TA, et al. Effect of crisis response planning vs. contracts for safety on suicide risk in U.S. Army soldiers: a randomized clinical trial. *J Affect Disord.* 2017;212:64–72.

59
Normalize Challenges
Validate That Treatment Is Difficult for Many Patients

Setting

Patients grow frustrated and disappointed when treatment does not go as they feel it should. This frustration eventually becomes overwhelming, limits receptivity to treatment recommendations, and saps the patient's motivation. A sense of isolation, inefficacy, and demoralization creeps in. The clinician can help the patient by providing a broader perspective and validating that many other patients have also struggled just as the patient is.

The Technique

When patients express disappointment that treatment is not progressing as hoped, convey how others have struggled similarly and how the patient is not alone in finding treatment difficult. One helpful sentiment to keep in mind is that if treatment were easy, the patient would not have come seeking help. Share optimism with the patient; emphasize that change and improvement are possible despite the hopelessness the patient may be experiencing in the moment.

Sample Dialogue

Patient: There's no point to this. I'm failing. It's hard. I want to quit.

Clinician: You are absolutely right, this is difficult. I really wish it were easier. Though if it were easy, you wouldn't have come for help!

Well that's true. I just wish I didn't feel so hopeless. No one understands how hard this is for me.

> I hear what you're saying. I can tell you that you are not the only patient who has felt this way. Many people struggle and find it difficult. You are definitely not alone.

> How do people handle it? I just want to give up.

> Even though it's difficult, I can tell you that it's possible to get better, and many people do.

Why This Works

The heart of this technique is validating the patient's experience. Validation, as defined in dialectical behavior therapy, is empathy plus the communication that the patient's perspective makes sense.[1] In this technique, the clinician voices an empathic understanding of the patient's frustration and also accepts that perspective as sensible in the circumstances, even going so far as to state they have worked with other patients who felt similarly in similar circumstances.

Some patients feel that they must protect the clinician from their hesitancies or doubts, lest the clinician lose interest in them as a patient. Through this technique, the clinician shares that not only will they not abandon the struggling patient but also that they have helped other patients who have felt how the patient is currently feeling. Normalizing the challenges of treatment reinforces the importance of the therapeutic relationship as a source of support.

In the sample dialogue, the clinician describes other patients' experience in a very general sense. The clinician must protect other patients' confidentiality and should be careful not to draw too explicit a parallel that would identify another patient. But the clinician can proffer some specifics aimed at the patient's background, for example, "other patients with families," or "other students I've worked work with." These phrases remain sufficiently broad yet still appropriate and useful. Many patients forget—or never realize—that others have travelled the same path as them.

The concept of demoralization has been used to describe how patients struggle in the face of illness and treatment.[2] Unlike patients with major depression, demoralized patients do not have consistently poor moods and are not anhedonic. Rather, demoralized patients primarily struggle with existential questions raised through the course of illness and treatment: Does anyone understand how I feel? What is important to me? Will I get better? What happens if I die? Illness is an isolating and frightening experience. This technique allows the clinician to connect the patient not only to the clinical relationship but also with a broader community of persons who have shared the patient's course. Helping the patient feel their perspective is understood can be as strongly validating as having shared the actual experience of illness.[3]

Final Thoughts

This technique has a clear role for patients who are openly struggling with treatment, but clinicians might consider it as well for patients whose difficulties are less transparent. For example, a patient may begin missing appointments or become newly non-adherent. These signs suggest additional struggles that the patient may be reluctant to share. The clinician's validation signals that the clinical relationship is a safe one in which to address these concerns.

The clinician should also keep in mind that numerous patient and community support groups are available that can further normalize and ameliorate the challenges of illness. These peer relationships can provide other practical support or perspective that would be inappropriate from a clinician, such as looser boundaries around communication. Table 59.1 lists a few well-recognized patient support groups with a national presence; patients may also find support through local religious groups, hospitals, and online platforms. In introducing these groups to the patient, the clinician can share their own thoughts of the groups' value and follow-up by asking about the patient's experience at the next appointment. Referring to patient support groups also helps the clinician share some of the burden for providing emotional support to the patient and returns some agency to the patient—"Here is another source of help you can take advantage of."

Table 59.1 National patient support groups

Condition	Supports
Alcohol use disorder	For patients: Alcoholics Anonymous www.aa.org For patients' family and friends: Al-Anon www.al-anon.org
Amphetamine use disorder	Crystal Meth Anonymous www.crystalmeth.org
Cancer	American Cancer Society www.cancer.org
Grief and bereavement	GriefShare www.griefshare.org
Lung disease	American Lung Association www.lung.org
Mental illness	National Alliance on Mental Illness www.nami.org
Opioid use disorder	Narcotics Anonymous www.na.org

References

1. Koerner K. *Doing Dialectical Behavior Therapy*. New York, NY: Guilford Press; 2012.
2. Griffith JL, Gaby L. Brief psychotherapy at the bedside: countering demoralization from medical illness. *Psychosomatics*. 2005;46(2):109–116.
3. Goldstein NJ, Vezich IS, Shapiro JR. Perceived perspective taking: when others walk in our shoes. *J Pers Soc Psychol*. 2014;106(6):941–960.

60

Reinforce the Positive

Encourage Healthy Decision-Making and Adherence With Plentiful Encouragement

Setting

Many clinical encounters revolve around patients' decision-making: decisions around treatment, decisions around medication adherence, decisions to start or stop certain behaviors. Sometimes the clinician has a single opportunity to influence a patient's decision—as in an emergency department—and sometimes the conversation is ongoing, as in a primary care clinic. Regardless of setting, the clinician must have techniques for guiding the patient in making healthy choices.

The Technique

Encourage healthy decision-making by continually lauding positive decisions, behaviors, and progress. The form of positive reinforcement depends on the situation. Agitated patients who are engaged in verbal de-escalation can be thanked for following directions or lowering their voice. Patients ambivalent around substance use should be applauded for even small steps toward reducing their use. Patients struggling with medication adherence deserve recognition for their success more than a review of barriers to timely refills.

Sample Dialogue

Clinician: Your blood pressure was pretty high today. What do you think is going on?

Patient: I have definitely not been good about taking my medication, that's for sure. But I did take them before coming in today.

That's great that you took it today. How come you haven't been good about taking your medication?

> I think I just forget. There is just so much to do in the morning, making breakfast for the kids, getting ready for work. I put the pill bottle in my bathroom last week, but that didn't really help.

> That is a busy morning. Good thinking moving that pill bottle somewhere where it's easier to remember. It's also great that you're brainstorming other ideas. Perhaps I can offer a few ideas myself?

Why This Works

As clinicians working with patients struggling with behavior change, we have no sticks—only carrots. Coercion has no place in most clinician-patient relationships and, regardless, there is no practical way to enforce behavior change. Even involuntarily treated inpatients will eventually have to make their own decisions after discharge. In light of this dynamic, many approaches have been developed for clinicians to sway patients' ambivalence in decision-making.

The patient's right decision does not guarantee success, however.

This technique is valuable for patients who have made the commitment to change but are nonetheless having difficulty realizing that change. The clinician must be the patient's partner in making healthier decisions. Any success or effort the patient describes is an opportunity for the clinician to offer praise. In the above dialogue, the patient describes one instance of adherence, one attempt to improve adherence, and a general interest in taking hypertension medication more regularly—the clinician makes separate, supportive statements for each. The clinician also validates the patient's account of how difficult adherence can be.

Positive reinforcement is powerfully motivating for changing behaviors. Even when punishment is an option, it is far less effective than positive reinforcement for changing behaviors. For example, parent management training (PMT) is a behavioral therapy designed to help parents manage problematic behaviors in children.[1] Parents have the ability to both reward and punish, but PMT focuses on the need for continued positive reinforcement rather than punishment.

Another reason to introduce more positive reinforcement into the interview is that it helps both clinician and patient feel good about the visit. By necessity, clinical encounters center around illness and difficulty. In a study of clinicians who work with pediatric cancer patients, the sense of always delivering bad news and being at odds with patients and families led to decreased clinician satisfaction and greater burnout.[2] Even in this challenging clinical situation, clinicians felt rewarded by positive and collaborative relationships. When patients have difficulty, it falls to the clinician to introduce a positive, encouraging energy to the treatment relationship.

Final Thoughts

Regardless of whether a patient relationship comprises a single encounter or many years, this technique is helpful for patients seeking change as well as clinicians who feel powerless to help realize that change. Change does not happen immediately, but it certainly can happen. Change is more likely when the clinician offers liberal praise for healthy behaviors. Clinicians who work in teams should also consider the value of positive reinforcement for supporting co-workers and encouraging change in the workplace.

References

1. Kazdin AE. *Parent Management Training: Treatment for Oppositional, Aggressive, and Antisocial Behavior in Children and Adolescents*. New York, NY: Oxford University Press; 2005.
2. Klassen A, Gulati S, Dix D. Health care providers' perspectives about working with parents of children with cancer: a qualitative study. *J Pediatr Oncol Nurs*. 2012;29(2):92–97.

Index

Note: Page numbers in **bold** indicate a table on the corresponding page.

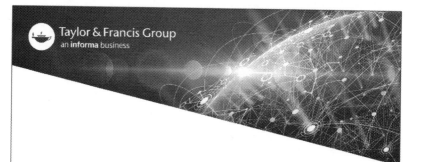

Printed in the United States
by Baker & Taylor Publisher Services